David Livin

David Livingstone was one of the greatest explorers who ever lived. His exciting exploits in Africa tell a story of unsurpassed courage and determination.

At first, it looked like David Livingstone would spend his life in the little town of Blantyre, Scotland. At age ten he began working in the cotton spinning mill. His workday began at 6 a.m. The ending whistle didn't sound until 8 p.m. After work he attended school for two hours.

He was told he'd never escape the daily toil of the cotton mill. Yet with only slight formal education, he succeeded in gaining admission to college. He studied to be a medical missionary. He attended a lecture by Robert Moffat, who was from Africa. Robert Moffat said, "I have sometimes seen, in the morning sun, the smoke of a thousand villages, where no missionary has ever been."

The phrase "the smoke of a thousand villages" caught David's imagination. He decided to go to Africa. Africa was being explored one cautious step at a time. David Livingstone made bold, sweeping trips far beyond the established line. Within a few months he'd gone deeper into Africa than any other missionary.

He left the comfortable missionary stations and lived with the African people. He learned their language. He treated their sick, helped them build a better life for themselves and told them about Jesus. He made plans to explore Africa, to preach the Gospel, and learn the scientific secrets of this great country.

David Livingstone described in vivid detail the unusual plants and animals of the African landscape. Using the same skills as a navigator on the ocean, he recorded his route into Africa so carefully it can be retraced today. His methods set a standard in the way exploration should be done.

As he grew more confident, David made a daring decision. He would cross from one side of Africa to the other. Many people said it couldn't be done. David had learned to think for himself and never give up. He said, "I will open a path into the interior or perish." How he succeeded against all the odds is an exciting story. Read on and let the adventure begin!

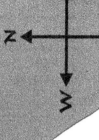

Suez Canal

Nile River

Lake Victoria

Congo River

AFRICA

LIVINGSTONE'S JOURNEYS:

——————— 1841

·········· 1842

· · · · · · 1849

– – – – 1850–1852

——————— 1852–1856

———·——· 1858–1863

–··–··–·· 1866–1869

–·–·–·– 1869–1873

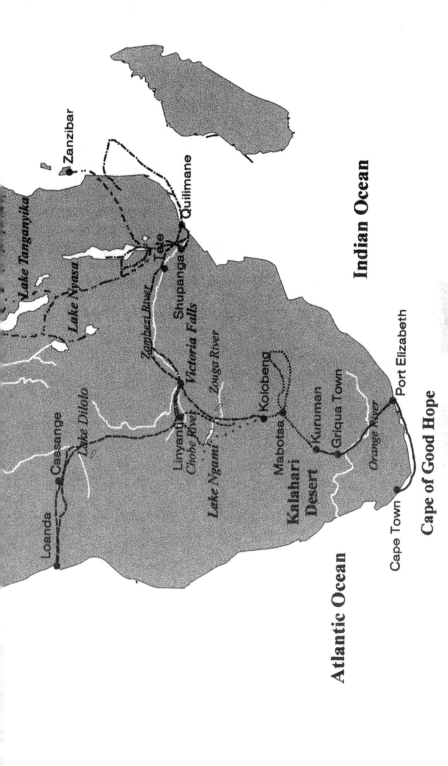

Lake Tanganyika

Zanzibar

Lake Nyasa

Quilimane

Indian Ocean

Tete

Shupanga

Zambezi River

Victoria Falls

Zouga River

Lake Dilolo

Cassange

Linyanti
Chobe River

Kolobeng

Lake Ngami

Mabotsa

Kuruman

Griqua Town

Kalahari
Desert

Orange River

Port Elizabeth

Loanda

Atlantic Ocean

Cape Town

Cape of Good Hope

ABOUT THE AUTHOR

John Hudson Tiner has been a science teacher, mathematician, and a cartographer (map maker). He is the author of more than 30 books. "I especially like to write biographies of famous people of the past," he says. "After I finish the research, a magic moment occurs when the story takes over. The characters come alive. No longer am I a writer. I become a time traveler who stands unseen in the shadows and reports the events as they take place."

Mr. Tiner is well known for his popular books about science and religion. Other Sowers Series books by Mr. Tiner include biographies of Isaac Newton, Johannes Kepler, Samuel F. B. Morse, Robert Boyle, and Louis Pasteur. He is also the author of several science textbooks.

John Hudson Tiner and his wife, Jeanene, live in High Ridge, Missouri. They have two children, John Watson and Lambda, and two grandchildren, Adam and Sydney.

ABOUT THE COVER ARTIST

We were fortunate to persuade Mr. William T. Hoetger to leave his semi-retirement and create our cover art. He is also known as artist "B. Hetch" for his extensive work in watercolors and pottery. Landscapes and still-life are among his favorite subjects. In the business world, Mr. Hoetger was president of Lettering Inc. of Michigan and also of Designs for Lettering International. He has served the Art Directors Club of Detroit as treasurer.

We thank him for his exceptional work in creating the cover for this book.

David Livingstone

African Explorer

by

John Hudson Tiner

Cover by **William Hoetger**

Illustrated by **Rebecca Booher**

MOTT
MEDIA

To Sydney Jeanene Stephens

Diane Davis and Joyce Bohn, Editors
William T. Hoetger, Cover Artist
Rebecca Booher, Illustrator

ISBN 0-88062-164-8

CONTENT

1	The Road to Africa	1
2	Smoke From a Thousand Villages	18
3	The Heart of Darkness	30
4	A Prospecting Trip	42
5	The Rainmaker	56
6	The Eyes of Death	68
7	Mabotsa: The Marriage Feast	81
8	The Land of Rivers and Trees	94
9	A Path to the Sea	106
10	The Raid on Kolobeng	118
11	A Man, a Gun or an Ox	130
12	The Smoke That Sounds	143
13	A Hundred Thousand Welcomes	156
14	The Last Journey	169
15	David Livingstone in Today's World	183
	Bibliography	193
	Index	195

ABOUT THE ILLUSTRATOR

"I have always been interested in drawing and creative things. When I was little I loved art class and craft time, especially when I could bring home gifts to my parents. At Hillsdale College I took many drawing classes, but also learned how to sculpt and oil paint. I particularly liked egg tempera painting because I made the paint out of raw egg yolks and color pigment. Since college, I have used my artistic skills in several different areas. While living at home in Syracuse, New York, I designed T-shirts, a brochure, and several logos. I later spent six months in Dallas, Texas working on book covers and CD rom covers that would be used by Wycliffe Bible Translators in various mission fields. I also touched up illustrations to be used in translated versions of the Bible all over the world. When I returned to New York, I worked on another brochure and many medical illustrations for pharmaceutical manuals. I recently moved to Michigan and took advantage of the opportunity to illustrate this book. While reading it, I learned many interesting facts about David Livingstone and his difficult, yet spiritually rewarding way of life. This knowledge helped me decide how to correctly portray many of his meetings, journeys, and discoveries. I hope the drawings I have done will add to your enjoyment of this book and help you better understand David Livingstone and the great things he did for God."

Rebecca Booher

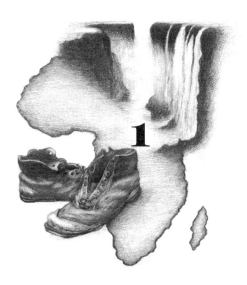

The Road to Africa

The headmen of the African village of Mabotsa came to Doctor David Livingstone. "Help us," they cried. "The lions have become more bold. They are attacking the village in open daylight. If you kill one of them the others will leave us alone."

David gave the natives courage. "You are perfectly able to kill one of the lions, but I will come with you."

The hunting party surrounded the lions on a hill outside the village. As the warriors closed in on the animals, David Livingstone noticed one that had slipped through their ring. He lifted his gun and fired at it.

As he paused to reload, a lion sprang upon him. Its powerful jaws crunched down on his shoulder. David could hear and feel the bones breaking. The lion snatched him up and shook him the way a dog shakes a rat.

David could not move or fight back. He turned

around and looked into the eyes of the lion—the eyes of death.

The road to Africa for David Livingstone had begun in Scotland where he was born on March 19, 1813. In 1823 he turned ten years old. He began work at the Blantyre Cotton Mill as a piecer. He walked back and forth between the reels of clattering spinning machines. He looked for broken threads. When he spotted one, he climbed between the whirling machinery and twisted together the ends of the broken thread.

His day at the mill began at 6 a.m. and ended at 8 p.m. The mill gave thirty minutes off for breakfast and an hour break for lunch. He worked twelve and one half hours each day. David tended a line of spinning jennies. The machine wove cotton thread into fabric. Hundreds of cotton threads fed into the machine. They often broke. It was David's job to quickly twist the broken ends back together.

The man in charge was called a spinner. He told David, "Watch carefully. Let no broken ends get by."

David kept moving, climbing over or crawling under the machinery. He guessed he would walk twenty miles before the day was over.

The mill was steam heated even in the summer. The managers believed cotton spun to better thread at a warm temperature. They kept the spinning room at a temperature between 80 and 90 degrees Fahrenheit. In the evening as it grew dark, one of the piecers, a girl, took a moment to sit down and rest. Exhausted and weary in the warm air, she soon fell asleep. The spinner saw the sleeping girl. He picked up a bucket of water and doused her with it. She sputtered awake.

David managed to stay awake. How would he fare after months of doing the same tasks over and over? Would he be able to stay awake? He needed something to occupy his mind and keep him alert.

The factory whistle sounded. His shift ended. But his day was not done. The mill children trudged to school. It was in a building outside the mill grounds to the east. The teacher greeted them. He had a smooth, pink face, bald head on top, but with thick side whiskers that went under his chin. His name was Mr. William MacSkimming.

He welcomed David and the other new students. "As you know, the Factory Act of 1802 requires mill owners to give free schooling to their child laborers. Blantyre Mill has hired me to provide this service. My classes will start as soon as the work is over. The class period will last for two hours—until 10 p.m."

One of the students asked, "Do you give homework?"

"Yes, indeed," Mr. MacSkimming said.

The students groaned. They were worn out before the class began.

David stayed up late that night to complete his assignments. At midnight, his mother took his books away. She turned out his lantern.

"I need more time to study," David protested.

"You need sleep, too," she said.

The next morning David carried one of his textbooks to work with him. He propped up the book on a frame of one of the machines. He would study as he worked.

As he passed by the book he read a sentence. He thought about it, memorized it, and then came back to grab another sentence. Despite the roar of the machinery, he kept up constant study. In this way he passed his time. Soon he received his first week's earnings.

David's father was a tea peddler. The man did not

earn a great deal of money. David gave most of his week's pay to his mother. He did keep a little. He waited for the bookseller. The man came around on payday with a case of books.

David asked, "Did you find a used copy of a Latin grammar for me?"

"Yes," the man said. He carried the crate slung by a leather strap over his shoulder. He set down the box and presented the book.

David read the title, "*Rudiments of the Latin Tongue.* Plain and easy introduction to Latin grammar." It had been published in Edinburgh in MDCCXCIII. David worked out the Roman numerals, 1793. "This book is thirty years old."

The man said, "You asked for a used book."

David bought the book to study as he worked. As the weeks passed he bought other books such as *Pilgrim's Progress*, *Paradise Lost*, travel stories and books about missionaries.

It amused the other mill workers to see a person so determined to study. The mill girls pitched bobbins at his book on the spinning jenny. They had great fun trying to knock it down.

Many children did not enroll in the mill school. Those that did often dropped out after they had learned to read and write. David did well in the school. Mr. MacSkimming offered an extra class in Latin. "This language is used by scholars, lawyers and doctors," he explained. David took the course and did well in it.

Some of the boys resented his success. "You study too much," they told him.

David ignored their comments. He knew education would be a way out of a lifetime of toil at the mill.

One of the older boys had quit school. He and his

friends spent their time after work playing darts and drinking at the tavern.

The older boy said, "I think you—"

"You think!" David interrupted. "I can think and act for myself. I don't need anybody to think for me."

With work and school David had little leisure time. Sometimes the steam engines that ran the mill broke down and gave him an unexpected holiday. He liked the summer evenings, too. The sun did not set until well after the mill let out. With no school in session, David had time to roam the countryside around Blantyre. He scrambled across the steep hills and valleys. Along the way he stopped to identify wildflowers, plants and herbs. He collected those he did not recognize.

Back home, he pored over reference books until he learned their names. He found mystery plants in either Rev. William Patrick's *The Indigenous Plants of Lanarkshire* or in Culpepper's *Herbal*.

The Livingstone family were readers. They always found room in their tiny apartment for books. Both David and his father read the Bible and books about the Bible. They enjoyed books on travel. David tried to interest his father in science, too. His father avoided the topic. When David brought home science books, his father would have nothing to do with them. He had a fear of books of science. He believed them unfriendly to Christianity.

When David expressed an interest in science, Neil Livingstone warned him against such a career. "How can you be a scientist and fulfill your promise to serve God?"

David, his father and the rest of the family attended Hamilton Church. It was three miles away.

They walked to the service each Sunday. During the break between morning and afternoon service the members of the congregation who lived nearby opened their homes to those who came from a distance. Mrs. Livingstone welcomed the hospitality. However, she always brought food for her family. She only asked for a place to sit at the table and hot water for tea.

At church, the preacher John Moir encouraged the congregation in their Christian duty to serve others. He taught, "Christians should have love for other human beings, have pity for suffering and concern for a person's physical and spiritual welfare."

David considered his religious education as important as any other. For five months, he studied under Arthur Anderson, one of the deacons at Hamilton Church.

Arthur Anderson told David, "The salvation of human beings ought to be the chief desire and aim of every Christian."

David often thought about the activities that competed for his attention: church, family, factory and his interest in travel and science. How could he satisfy all of these conflicting demands?

One day he read a book by Dr. Thomas Dick, *Philosophy of a Future State*. In the book, Dr. Dick proposed the idea that science and Scripture were not foes of one another. David put aside the book. "Why, of course," David thought. "Nature and Scripture have the same author—God."

David wrote to the author of the book. Dr. Dick was a retired minister of the Gospel and amateur astronomer. He lived in Dundee, Scotland, about 80 miles from Blantyre. During one of his rare holidays David visited the good doctor in person.

The man's house showed that the doctor was no

ordinary individual. Scotland often had low lying fog that ruined telescopic seeing. Doctor Dick had hauled in eight thousand barrel loads of earth to form a mound. He built his home and observatory on the miniature mountain. It was a more suitable site for star gazing.

David told about his father's view of science. "Some Christians will have nothing to do with science," David said. "They say it is ungodly. Some parents actually refuse to let their children study science. They fear it will damage their Christian beliefs."

Dr. Thomas Dick said, "Many people do try to keep their children ignorant about science. I oppose such measures. Look at the glory of the heavens and the beauty of nature. They confirm the existence of a Maker."

The visit with the good doctor convinced David to become a scientist. About the only science in which a person could earn a living was medicine. David decided to become a doctor. The first obstacle to this decision was his father who had to approve his plans.

"Medicine must serve a religious purpose," his father said. "Only if you put your medical training to a specific religious purpose will I support you."

One day David Livingstone picked up a religious tract brought home from the Hamilton Church by his father. Karl Gutzlaff, a missionary to China, had written the tract. He appealed for more missionaries. Karl Gutzlaff explained that people in foreign lands opened their borders to missionaries with skills as carpenters, metal workers and craftsmen. Doctors were especially welcome.

David investigated further. Karl Gutzlaff worked as a missionary in Canton, China. The Netherlands Missionary Society sponsored him. Karl Gutzlaff learned the Chinese language and dressed as they did.

China was a vast country with a huge population almost totally devoid of missionaries.

David found that his father had heard of Karl Gutzlaff. The year before, the China missionary had written a book, *Three Journeys along the Coast of China.* Neil Livingstone had read the book. He approved of it.

David discussed his proposal to be a medical missionary with his mother and father. David said, "I can be both a medical doctor and a missionary!"

Neil Livingstone hesitated. "That a missionary can also be a doctor is a new and untried idea. I fear such a dual career will divide your attention from the essential task—preaching the Gospel."

As time passed, Mr. Livingstone saw his son's determination. He withdrew his objection and actively supported his boy. Neil Livingstone said, "What you propose is a practical way to combine science and religion."

David could not believe his good fortune. His three great passions were the spread of the Gospel, science and travel. As a medical missionary to a foreign country, he'd be able to achieve all three goals.

Now that he had his father's blessing, the next obstacle was money. College tuition for one semester would be 12 pounds. He also had to rent a room near the school and pay for food and other living expenses. David shared his plans with John Moir, the minister at Hamilton.

"How shall you pay for college tuition?" the minister asked. He suggested that David seek help from a missionary society. "Missionary societies select suitable candidates and provide a salary so they can devote themselves full time to their mission work. They will even pay for your education."

David had already explored that idea and dismissed it. He attended Hamilton Church because it was an independent congregation. He enjoyed religious freedom. Suppose he received aid from a missionary society. He'd have to subscribe to the beliefs of the church denomination that supported him. Missionary societies strictly controlled what their members could and could not teach.

David told John Moir, "I believe it is better to pay my own way and thus stay independent."

At the end of the summer in 1836, David counted his money. He announced to his father, "I'll be able to start at Anderson's College this fall."

Early on a cold morning late in 1836, Neil Livingstone and his son walked the eight miles to Glasgow. Heavy snow covered the ground. They took with them a list of likely lodgings drawn up by a friend at the Hamilton Church.

The list proved a disappointment. One by one, they struck the locations from the list. Many of the rooms were already rented. Some were in a bad part of town. Others were too far from school. Most were too expensive. Father and son grew cold and tired.

All around them the city bustled with activity. The industrial revolution had come to Glasgow. Factory chimneys pumped out thick black smoke. Powerful draft horses snorted in the cold air as they struggled to pull heavy wagons piled high with barrels and boxes.

They walked down to the shipyards. They rested for a while and watched the bustle of shipbuilding along the Clyde River.

The Livingstone apartment in Blantyre also offered a great view of the Clyde River. They lived in the top flat of a three-story building. David could see the factory, the constantly changing river and the groves of

oak and ash trees around the Bothwell estate in the distance.

As David and his father rested in Glasgow, David realized his family was fortunate to have such good lodging at the mill. Twenty-four families lived in the three-story building. Each family had a room fourteen by ten feet. In this space, David's family lived: father and mother Livingstone, sons John, David and Charles and daughters Janet and Agnes.

The room had two recessed alcoves for beds. Below the high beds were smaller beds, like shelves, that could be pulled out. At night, the little room would then become almost entirely covered with the beds.

When John and David became teenagers, they moved in with the grandparents in a nearby cabin. David's grandfather, a tailor, made clothes for the orphans who worked at the cotton mill. David's father had all kinds of rules for living a good and wholesome life. His grandfather gave much less advice. He would merely say, "Be honest."

David would now be moving out of his grandfather's house and into a new apartment in Glasgow—if Neil and David could find suitable lodging.

After their rest by the shipyards, father and son continued their search. The day was nearly gone when they came across a room that looked like it would do.

"What is the price?" David asked the landlady.

"Two shillings a week," she said.

The room was on Rotten Row and seemed overpriced. The woman said, "I am a poor widow, and room rent is my only income."

David took the room. He unpacked his belongings. He had brought some food—tea, sugar and other items for a light meal.

The next morning he reported to the college. As he entered the building two other students who had attended before greeted him. The two young men were William Thomson and Lyon Playfair. When they learned he was new they gave him a tour of the college. They ended the tour at the laboratory of James Young. He was the assistant to the chemistry professor. James Young was in charge of the chemistry laboratory.

James Young welcomed David. To all three he said, "I have the material for the improved galvanic battery."

William Thomson said, "Let me put it together for you." William Thomson quickly made the electric battery. He showed how the completed circuit would cause a spark when the wires touched together. As he watched his two new friends, David realized he had a lot to learn. He felt lucky to have met the two students. They were humble and eager to learn.

Finally, they stopped their electrical experiments to register for the fall term. David's friends showed him the way and let him go first. The college official took extra care to be helpful with David and the two other boys. When he finished, the man asked, "Do my lords require anything else?"

David smiled at the man's joke. David was a mill worker, not royalty. His two friends took the man seriously. Lyon Playfair said politely, "No, thank you."

David held back and whispered a question to the college official. "Who are those two boys?"

The college official said, "Lord Playfair and his friend. They are both members of royalty."

Later, David learned that William Thomson's royal name was Lord Kelvin. Despite being a student, William Thomson had already written a research paper on mathematics and it was read by the Royal Society of Edinburgh.

David attended Dr. Thomas Graham's class in chemistry and Dr. Andrew Buchanan's medical lectures. He also studied Greek and the Bible.

That evening he returned to his room. He considered himself fortunate to have met the two lords and James Young, the chemistry assistant. They all were alive with a sense of curiosity.

David made a cup of tea. The tin of tea was nearly half empty. He thought he had packed more. As he settled back in the wooden chair, it creaked. The noise sounded loud in the lonely room. He was not used to studying in such quiet surroundings. He missed his family.

On Saturday he walked home to spend the weekend with his family. He told his sister, "I'll need some more tea and sugar before I go back."

Janet said, "I thought you had enough to last for several weeks."

David said, "During the week, my supply was reduced mysteriously. Another boarder explained the mystery to me. Our landlady sneaks into our rooms when we are out and helps herself to our tea and sugar. I cannot believe that a person who is poor would use that as an excuse to steal. Our father has earned a meager living all of his life selling tea. He's been in and out of hundreds of homes and businesses. Yet, he would not think of stealing from his customers. Instead, he leaves behind religious tracts."

David did move to a room on High Street. The comfortable room was only a few shillings more. The landlady did not steal from her tenants.

David successfully completed his first college session in Glasgow in April 1837. He quickly returned home to spend his summer vacation hard at work at the cotton mill. David had worked for a year and a half to attend the first session. For the next session, which began in the fall, he would have only the summer months to earn the money he needed.

As time grew closer to begin his second term, David counted his savings. It was not going to be enough. His father came forward with some money that he claimed David had earned himself. "Remember the summer you and your sister collected flowers and biological samples. You were paid a small sum for them by an herb collector. I set the money aside for such an emergency."

David could remember collecting the herbs. He had tramped all over the countryside. Janet complained bitterly that he had walked her legs off. Yet, each morning she had been ready to go again with him. He was pretty sure he had long ago spent any money from the herb collecting. The money came from savings all right, from his father's small savings.

Even that wouldn't be enough. He had to borrow a little more from his brother John. He would have just enough to finish the next session at Glasgow.

During the summer David Livingstone kept in touch with his friends by writing letters. He was especially happy when the British mail service introduced the penny stamp. Before then when he wrote, the person who received the letter had to pay the postage. He hesitated to write too often, thinking his friend would resent paying so much postage. Now, he could mail letters to everyone and the burden would be his, rather than theirs.

He also made time for long walks with Arthur Anderson, his friend from Hamilton Church. Arthur Anderson was a deacon at the church. He gave religious instruction to David. They had gone beyond teacher and student to become close friends.

David told his friend, "By working at the mill in the summer I can almost support myself while attending college next fall."

"Almost?" Arthur Anderson asked.

"Despite my best efforts, I am putting a strain on the family finances. I need an additional source of income," David said.

Arthur Anderson asked, "Why not ask for aid from a missionary society? Suppose you do succeed in earning a medical degree? Your goal may still be out of reach. You must travel to China or wherever you decide to go. You will have to start a mission station and support yourself and your wife in a foreign country."

David said, "A wife? I have no plans to get married."

Arthur Anderson said, "Most missionaries take wives. It is expected of you."

"Not me," Livingstone said.

"In any case the expenses for you alone in a foreign country will be more than your schooling itself."

David Livingstone nodded. His friend had a point. Karl Gutzlaff had been supported in China by a missionary society.

Arthur Anderson said, "The London Missionary Society is nonsectarian, much like the church in Hamilton. They have missionaries all over the world— China, India, the islands in the South Pacific, the West Indies and Africa."

David still hesitated. "I have been accustomed to make my own way. It is not quite agreeable to become dependent on others."

John Moir, the minister at the Hamilton Church, learned of David's indecision. He took the first step. He wrote to the society in August. The information they sent convinced David to give them a try. David applied the next month, shortly before he returned to Glasgow for more medical studies.

The London Missionary Society did not immediately answer. Three months passed. In January, 1838, they sent an application package. David would be judged on his written answers to seventeen questions.

One of the questions asked, "What do you understand are the proper duties of a Christian missionary?"

David labored to compose an answer to this important issue. He wrote, "A Christian missionary should endeavor by every means in his power to make known the Gospel by preaching, exhortation, conversation, instruction of the young; improving, so far as in his power, the conditions of those among whom he labors, by introducing the arts and sciences of civilization, and doing everything in his power to commend Christianity to their hearts and consciences."

Another of the questions related to marriage. He was well aware that many missionary societies encouraged their members to be married. A team, they believed, would do better than a single individual. David could have stepped lightly around this question. Instead, he boldly decided to let them know exactly where he stood—he had no intention of marrying.

David wrote, "Unmarried; under no engagement relating to marriage; never made proposals of marriage; nor conducted myself so to any woman as to cause her to suspect that I intended anything related to marriage."

David mailed the answers to London. The society director examined the answers, which puzzled him.

David's answers were brisk and abrupt. They were rough hewn and did not flow. The young man wrote in choppy phrases. His choices of words were clumsy. On the other hand, the ideas behind the words were original. David Livingstone could *think*.

David waited for a reply to his application. None came. He finished the second session at Glasgow. Back to Blantyre he came. He returned to the daily toil of the cotton mill. Slowly the summer passed.

For months he'd been in an agony of indecision about whether to apply to a missionary society. It had never crossed his mind that they might also have misgivings about him. Would they accept him?

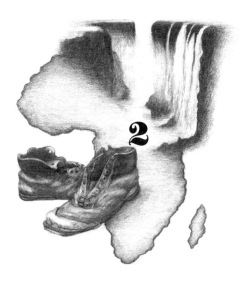

Smoke From a Thousand Villages

Neil Livingstone fumed. His son, David, was an excellent choice for a missionary. Why couldn't the London Missionary Society see that fact!

He thought of all the important facts the society should know about David. Shortly before starting to work at the mill, David memorized Psalm 119. It had 176 verses, the longest of the Psalms. Even as a young boy, David worked long hours in the mill. When the closing whistle sounded, most children were too tired for study. Despite aching muscles and exhausted bodies, David and a few others stumbled to the mill school for two hours of classes.

What pleased Neil Livingstone the most was David's faith. Any success would be incomplete without a love for God.

Neil Livingstone wrote a letter to the Director of the London Missionary Society. He told about David's struggle for an education. He pointed out that David completed his Latin class, although everyone else dropped out.

He also described David's determination to make the most of his education. "David came home on the week-end. A neighbor, Fergus Ferguson, offered David a ride to Glasgow on Monday morning. To take the easy ride in the carriage would make him late for the first class. David instead woke up early and walked so he'd arrive in time for the first lecture."

Neil asked one final favor of the Director. He assured them that he had not told his son he was writing. "I would rather he never knew, since he would certainly disapprove."

Even Neil Livingstone's letter caused no quick reply.

Finally, the Director invited David to London. Fergus Ferguson offered a loan for the fare and David agreed. The Director interviewed him on August 13, 1838. A week later he called him back to talk to him again. The society was having a difficult time deciding upon him.

David Livingstone did not have the polish of an accomplished speaker. His voice was thick and sometimes hard to understand. He tended to be brief, going to the heart of the matter. He seldom gave examples or asides that made for an interesting talk.

Yet, the Director could not bring himself to reject David out right. He said, "Scholarship is fine, but we look for well-rounded individuals who do more than preach. We have decided to put you on probation for three months while you receive preacher training. You must pass this training to be a preacher before you can go on to medical school and travel to a foreign country."

What would be his salary? David wondered.

"We are supported by poor people's shillings rather than the pounds of the rich," the Director said. "Our single missionaries receive 75 pounds a year."

David was aware that Dutch missionary societies paid their missionaries 400 to 500 pounds a year. Yet, he did not complain. The 75 pounds was a fabulous sum after his struggles to raise 12 pounds for medical school at Glasgow. Imagine, they would actually pay more for him to attend school than he'd earned at his mill job.

In London David met Joseph Moore, another student. On Sunday they attended three places of worship. Then on Tuesday they visited Westminster Abbey, a famous church more than a thousand years old.

Joseph said, "British sovereigns have been crowned here. See the stone under the coronation chair. That's the Stone of Scone, where Scottish kings were crowned. All around are the graves of kings, queens, and famous British subjects."

David Livingstone stopped at the monument to Isaac Newton and pointed it out to his new friend.

His three months probation would be at Chipping Ongar in Essex. He would study classic literature and learn how to write sermons. David and six other students shared a building. They did their own cooking and housekeeping.

The young men's instructor was Richard Cecil who lived down the road. He taught out of his house. Mr. Cecil taught Greek, Latin, Hebrew and lesser known points of theology.

Although David struggled to satisfy Cecil, he

had a vague uneasiness about the usefulness of the classes. Joseph Moore would be sailing to Tahiti to bring the Gospel to Pacific Islanders. D. G. Watt would go to India. Walter Inglis would teach the primitive tribes in Africa. David thought he would be going to China. Cecil prepared students to preach at university towns, not native villages.

One area Richard Cecil equipped David for was his missionary work. He taught him how to learn languages, how to sound out words using phonics and to detect the parts of speech and build a grammar. It was the most useful skill he learned from Richard Cecil.

One Sunday after the morning worship, Richard Cecil sent for David.

"Mr. Livingstone, do you have your sermon memorized?" the man asked.

"Yes," David said. He tapped the folded paper in his coat pocket. "It is the one you have seen and corrected."

Richard Cecil said, "The minister at Stanford Rivers has fallen sick after the morning service. You shall preach there tonight."

David reviewed the sermon again. When the time came, he took the pulpit and looked out at the small congregation. Suddenly he realized he could not remember a word of the sermon. It had all fled his mind. He could not even recall the subject.

David took a deep breath. He said, "Friends, I have forgotten all I had to say." He ran from the chapel.

Joseph Moore and D. G. Watt knew that their friend was struggling.

"Cecil thinks he's too rough and blunt." D. G. Watt said, "What do you think he will recommend?"

"David is on probation," Joseph Moore said. "I think rejection is a real possibility."

Richard Cecil gave his decision to the Director of the missionary society, "I feel obligated to report unfavorably. Mr. Livingstone is ungainly in movement, slow and indistinct in speech. He will not do, I think, for a preacher. And as a pastor or evangelist, I doubt if he could win those around him."

The Director hesitated to send such a determined person home. He did not entirely agree with Richard Cecil. The Director asked, "Where are his failings?"

Richard Cecil said, "He has a heavy manner and rustic style. He is plodding. His accent grates on the ears of an educated audience, and he is still lacking in knowledge."

A member of the Director's board spoke in David's favor. "If Mr. Livingstone is not ready because of a lack of training, we can give him more time."

"Very well," the Director said, "I will extend his probation for additional training."

After the second session, Richard Cecil raised the same objections. This time he added, "Mr. Livingstone gives me pleasure in some important respects. He has sense and quiet vigor. His temper is good and his character substantial. I do not like the thought of rejecting him. He is a diligent, staunch, single-hearted laborer. I say accept him."

David had passed his religious education. He would next need to pass his medical examination. David returned to London on January 2, 1840 to work toward a medical degree. At Glasgow, the medical studies had been almost entirely from books. In London he had hands-on experience in the practical side of medicine, including attending patients. He lodged with other students at Mrs. Sewell's Boarding House on Aldersgate Street.

One day the students gathered in the sitting room to greet an important visitor. He was Robert Moffat, a famous South African missionary. He had a great bushy beard and sharp penetrating eyes. He stood six feet tall and walked with a vigorous stride. He dominated the room when he walked into it.

The man said, "I've been a missionary to Africa for twenty-three years. I'm on leave to England for a year with my family. When I learned missionaries in training boarded here, I came to introduce myself and urge you to consider Africa."

David learned that Robert Moffat was 44 years old. Like Livingstone, he was from Scotland and from a poor family. Robert Moffat went to Africa in the fall of 1817. Since 1824, the missionary had been working at Kuruman, far to the north of any other stations. One could get there only by traveling 500 miles overland by ox cart. The journey began at Port Elizabeth at the southern tip of Africa. The trek took two months.

Robert Moffat told about the present knowledge of Africa. "The heart of Africa is a mystery to the rest of the world. Coming down from northern Africa travelers are stopped by the great Sahara Desert. It spans the entire continent from the Atlantic Ocean to the Red Sea. From the south the Kalahari Desert acts as a barrier. Many people believe the Kalahari goes until it meets the Sahara.

"Travel is especially difficult in Africa. Few routes are established on land. On other continents rivers can be used for transportation. In Africa the rivers have their entrances clogged with sand bars. Past the mouths, the land rises to the African highlands. Boats that make it past the sand bars encounter strong currents and cataracts—stretches of rapids and waterfalls."

David was fascinated by the great man's stories. Robert Moffat had gone deeper into Africa than any other missionary or explorer. David Livingstone asked to meet privately with Mr. Moffat. He said, "Because of an interest in the books by Karl Gutzlaff, I'd assumed I would go to China. But the Opium War has closed that door."

Relations between Britain and China had fallen apart. To control trade in opium, a drug, the emperor had closed China's harbors to all British vessels. The Emperor accused some British leaders of working with the drug dealers. By 1840, when David came to London, the two countries were moving toward war with one another.

David said, "The London Missionary Society has decided not to risk sending any more missionaries to China until the war ends. It could drag on for years. I've about decided to seek a post elsewhere."

Robert Moffat said, "Has the London Missionary Society proposed another place?"

"Yes," David said. "This July they asked my feeling about the British West Indies. The abolition of slavery in British territory has caused many of the sugar plantations in the Caribbean to fail. The islands are in turmoil. The local natives face hard times."

Robert Moffat said, "Into such a place the right missionary could accomplish much good."

David said, "The islands are well supplied with medical men who settled there to earn a living. They would resent my free medical care and try to scare away my patients. Should someone become sick and die while under my care—which is bound to happen—

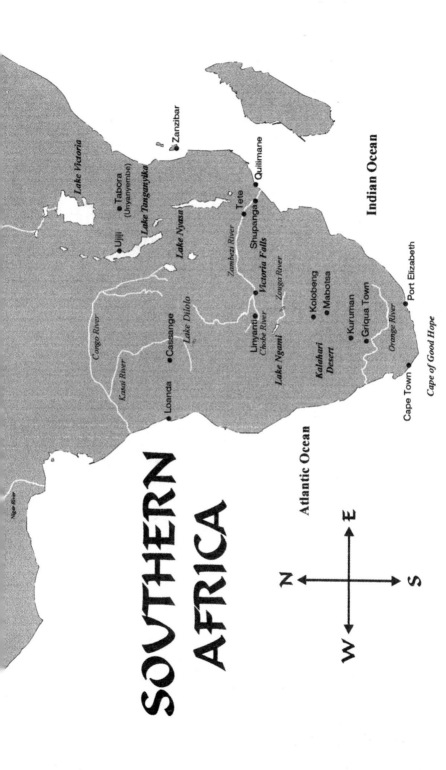

they would use it to destroy my reputation. I told the society that the West Indies was not right for me."

David said with real feeling, "I want to break new ground! Do you think I would do for Africa?"

Robert Moffat answered carefully. "Yes, you would do well provided you don't go to an established station, but advance to an unoccupied area."

"Is there opportunity beyond Kuruman?" David asked.

The great missionary to Africa said, "In the vast plain to the north I have sometimes seen, in the morning sun, the smoke of a thousand villages, where no missionary has ever been."

The smoke of a thousand villages.

That night David could not sleep. Robert Moffat's message burned in his mind. David thought, "What is the use of waiting for the end of this Opium War? Africa is my goal!"

Robert Moffat reported to his wife that he had interested at least one person in coming to Africa. "His name is David Livingstone from Scotland."

"Is he married?" Mrs. Moffat asked.

"No," Robert Moffat said.

"He will be lonely and miserable in South Africa without a wife," she predicted.

Her husband said, "Livingstone has no intention to marry. He has worked all of his life. He has had little time to make ordinary friends, much less pursue a lady to be his wife."

One of the Moffats' reasons for returning to civilization was their two daughters, Mary and Annie. Both were of marrying age. The visit to England would give their girls an opportunity to meet eligible bachelors. Perhaps they would find mates.

David knew that their eldest daughter was named

Mary. Although he visited with Robert Moffat often, he never had occasion to meet either one of their daughters.

David studied a map of Africa. Features along the coast had been marked and named. The heart of Africa was blank. David marveled that no missionaries, explorers or scientists had ventured into that vast unknown land. Imagine a world of mountains, deserts, rivers, lakes, strange plants and animals, human tribes as ancient as the land—all undiscovered and unstudied.

While in London David attended worship at the Silver Street Chapel in Falcon Square. There he met Risdon Bennet, a physician at the Aldersgate Street Dispensary. The good doctor made a special effort to plan David's medical training.

Dr. Bennet said, "The schedule is a rough one. You can make the rounds with me at Aldersgate Street Dispensary, attend lectures about diseases at the Charing Cross Dispensary. Also, I recommend you try to fit in a course in anatomy at the Hunterian Museum." Anatomy is the study of bones, muscles and organs of the body.

David also attended numerous lectures at the British and Foreign Medical School. He took courses in botany, the study of plants. He learned that doctors treated many tropical diseases with medicines extracted from plants.

At the Hunterian Museum, he met Richard Owen. Richard Owen originally intended to become a doctor. He earned a medical degree at the University of Edinburgh in Scotland. After graduation he began working at a museum of the Royal College of Surgeons. He had gone to Paris for further study. Now, he concentrated on comparative anatomy. He compared the same parts of different animals.

"Teeth, for instance, tell much about how an animal feeds and lives," he told David. "Animals that eat grass have large flat teeth for crushing and grinding their food. Animals that eat flesh have sharp teeth for cutting and ripping. From a single tooth you can tell a lot about an animal."

Richard Owen learned that David was going to Africa. "You must ship specimens back for me to study," Richard Owen insisted.

"What should I send?" David asked.

"Little is known beyond Mr. Moffat's station at Kuruman. Everything will be of value: bones, hides, seeds, bark, leaves."

While in London, David began reading two magazines. One was the *Lancet*, a journal for physicians. The other one was *Punch*, a humor magazine. He subscribed to both of them.

He could have taken his medical exam in either London or Glasgow. An examination for the medical degree at The Royal College of Surgeons in London was expensive. Instead he chose to be certified at the Faculty of Physicians and Surgeons in Glasgow.

He passed the test on November 16, 1840. With the medical degree safely earned, David checked the shipping schedule. He had enough time to spend one day with his family. He set out that afternoon for Blantyre. He gathered with his family around the fireplace in the little one room apartment. They talked late into the night. David mentioned that the London Missionary Society received most of its money from Christians who were not well to do.

Neil Livingstone told his son, "The time will come when rich men will think it an honor to support missionaries at foreign stations instead of spending their money on hounds and horses."

Around midnight his mother began putting away the dishes.

"I have but one night to be with you," David said. "Let's stay up later."

His mother smiled at the idea. "When you were ten I had to send you to bed at midnight so you would get enough sleep. Now you're a young man, but I still must tell you when it is time to go to sleep."

As so many times before, his mother packed him off to bed.

He awoke the next morning to find the sky overcast and the weather cold. The family got up at five o'clock. His mother fixed breakfast and the family prayed together. His father said, "Read from the Bible for us."

David Livingstone read Psalm 121. That Psalm ends with the words, "The LORD will keep you from all harm—he will watch over your life; the LORD will watch over your coming and going both now and forevermore."

He said good-bye to Charles, Janet, Agnes and his mother. Early in the morning David and his father set out to hike to Glasgow, to Broomielaw Quay. There he would catch the steamship to Liverpool.

David's family members were going their separate ways. John, his older brother, had already moved to Canada. Charles was making plans to go to the United States. David would trek five hundred miles into Africa to Moffat's station at Kuruman.

When Robert Moffat had left for Africa, he had stayed for 23 years. If David stayed as long, he would return as a man of fifty. Incredible! It was entirely possible he would never see his father or mother again. What changes would he find in Scotland when he returned? What adventures awaited him in Africa?

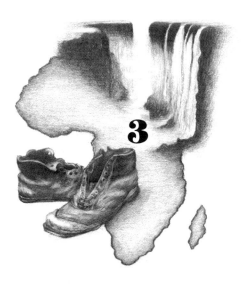

The Heart of
Darkness

As he passed through London, David Livingstone
attended a ceremony that officially ordained him as a
minister. He placed little importance on the ceremony.
For years, he had viewed himself as a disciple of Jesus
and a preacher of the Gospel. More important to him
were the papers from the London Missionary Society
that identified him as a missionary to Africa.

On December 8, 1840, he set sail aboard the
George under Captain Donaldson. David knew some
of the other passengers. Two of them he had met in
London: William Ross and his wife. William Ross was
a missionary, too. Like David he would travel to
Kuruman for field training with Robert Moffat.

David found William Ross pleasant enough.
However, he avoided whenever possible William Ross'
wife. She had an opinion about every matter. For
instance, she tried time and again while in London to

act as a matchmaker for David. She had introduced him to several women. Mrs. Ross urged David to marry.

The passengers went to their cabins below deck. Mrs. Ross took her husband's arm. She looked pleased with herself. She said pointedly to David, "Two is better than one."

David was left alone on the deck.

"Doctor Livingstone," someone called.

"Yes?" David asked. The man who called his name was Captain Donaldson.

The Captain said, "Welcome aboard the *George*. I understand you are interested in navigation."

"Yes, I am," David said. "I expect my occupation to take me into parts of Africa never before visited by Europeans. I would like to make a reliable map of my progress."

"Navigation is a skill that's not quickly mastered," the Captain said. "Once we are well underway, I will be happy to give you an introduction."

David Livingstone settled down to life aboard ship. He quickly learned how to sleep despite the swaying of the ship. He slept in a hammock. It canceled out some of the movement of the ship.

To pass the time David wrote letters to his family and friends at home. He ended his letters with a special request. "Have the kindness to remember me in your prayers," he wrote. "I won't forget you in mine."

David also enjoyed the company of Captain Donaldson. They talked about many subjects, including navigation.

"Finding your location at sea and on a broad, trackless desert are similar in many ways," the good Captain said. "The art of navigation is not an easy one.

You understand that any place on earth can be identified by latitude and longitude?"

David promptly replied, "Yes. Latitude is the distance north or south of the equator. Longitude is the distance east or west of the Prime Meridian, which goes through Greenwich, England."

Captain Donaldson said, "Latitude is the simplest of the two to calculate. Polaris is the star near the North Celestial Pole. If it is in the horizon, then we are exactly on the equator, or 0 degrees latitude. If it is directly overhead, then we are exactly at the North Pole, or 90 degrees north latitude."

"Where is Polaris now?" David asked.

"It fell below the horizon and out of sight when we crossed the equator. The brighter stars have had their positions accurately plotted on a star chart. Your latitude can be found by the angle that a known star makes above the southern horizon. Other sky objects can be used, too, such as the planets, moon and sun."

"How do you find the ship's longitude?" David asked.

"The stars alone do not reveal our distance east or west. For longitude we must have a clock that keeps accurate time." Captain Donaldson unlocked and carefully opened a wooden case. An expensive watch the size of a saucer rested inside. "I wind it myself the same time each day and to the same tension on the master spring. It must keep good time for all our weeks at sea. Every minute it gains or loses will throw us a mile off course for every day we sail."

Captain Donaldson continued, "The clock is set to Greenwich time. The difference between it and local time gives the longitude. Suppose our local time is eleven o'clock, but Greenwich time is twelve o'clock noon. The difference of one hour means we are 1/24 of the way around the earth from Greenwich. As you know, a full circle has 360 degrees. Taking 1/24 of 360 degrees gives 15 degrees. That's about a thousand miles."

David suspected navigation was more complicated than the Captain made it sound. He had read that the atmosphere caused stars near the horizon to appear higher than they actually were. He also knew that the paths of the sun and moon across the sky changed with the seasons. David asked the Captain about this.

"Yes," the Captain said, "a navigator must calculate corrections for all of these effects and apply them. Navigation is not learned in a night."

The Captain invited David to stay up with him to observe the moon with a quadrant.

David readily agreed. He was determined to learn as much about navigation as he could. The Captain showed him how to measure the angle between the moon and the horizon. They stayed up until midnight. David succeeded in measuring the moon's angle above the horizon. "At least on land it would be easier to hold the quadrant steady," he observed.

Captain Donaldson applied all the corrections. He announced, "Our position is 7 degrees south latitude, 18 degrees west longitude."

The Captain put away the quadrant in a padded box to protect it from damage. He checked the barometer. "The air pressure has been falling all day. A gale will overtake us." He began issuing commands to the crew.

The sky had been clear. Now in the moonlight, he saw dark and powerful clouds boiling up on the horizon.

The ship lifted and fell as it sailed through heavy swells. Many of the passengers had already become seasick. The waves tossed the ship about. A man and woman stumbled to the rail and turned their stomachs inside out.

David recognized the couple. They were Mr. and Mrs. Ross. David knew that nobody died of seasickness—they just felt like they might. The couple stumbled away from the rail to return to their cabin.

As they disappeared inside, David could not resist speaking to Mrs. Ross. "Remember," he said, "two is better than one!"

The storm grew worse. The Captain ordered passengers to be confined below decks. The ship creaked and groaned. Sailors brought in the sails. Wind howled through the rigging and empty masts. The ship lifted high and then plunged into the waves. Water washed over the bow. The ship twisted as if being shaken by a writhing sea serpent.

David said his prayers and tried to sleep. Suddenly a terrible thud came from the opposite side of the cabin. A trunk had broken free. It thudded to the floor and slid about. It crashed into everything in the cabin, knocking other items free. Since it was impossible to move around the cabin during the violent pitching, David stayed in his bunk, hung on, and rode out the storm.

By morning the storm had passed. David looked around the cabin. The escaped trunk had smashed everything else to pieces. He had never seen such a mess.

The *George* had not completely escaped the storm's fury. Captain Donaldson explained the problem to the passengers. "The gale split the foremast. We will be obliged to put into Rio de Janeiro for a new one. We will take on a fresh supply of water, too."

"Rio!" Mrs. Ross said. "Rio de Janeiro is in South America."

"Yes, it is," Captain Donaldson agreed patiently. "We will not be as far off course as you imagine. Our normal route would have brought us to within 200 miles of South America. We'll anchor in Rio only for as long as it takes for repairs."

David had set out for South Africa and ended up in South America instead! He could not contain his delight at the beautiful scenery. Soaring hills stood watch over one of the most beautiful harbors in the world. The lush greenery of the tropical rain forest carpeted the hillsides.

The imposing mountains and mysterious rain forest looked very near. David wanted to explore the delightful country, especially after seven weeks in the close quarters of the ship. Perhaps he could hike five or six miles into the forest.

Mrs. Ross was aghast at the idea. "You don't know what dangers lurk in the dark forest."

William Ross agreed with his wife. "I'm thankful to be on solid ground. We've already had enough adventure."

David decided to set out for the jungle. No one else aboard the ship dared to go exploring with him.

The route took him first through clearings with large plantations. Coffee, sugar and Indian corn grew in the fields. He passed well kept orchards of orange and cocoanut trees. The large plantations gave way to smaller farms. The road became steeper and less traveled. It narrowed into a cart path and finally a foot trail.

David stopped to get his breath and admire a butterfly. It was enormous. He also spied a grasshopper of gigantic size. Lizards darted out of sight when he brushed against a leaf. The great rain forest was so green it gave the very air itself a green tinge. Vegetation carpeted the ground, making it spongy. Mosses and ferns grew on the trees, vegetation upon vegetation.

Banana trees grew everywhere. Earlier he had noticed that natives used the broad banana leaves in a variety of ways, from wrapping paper to rain hats.

David had not eaten much fresh food aboard ship. Would the natives sell him some fresh fruit and vegetables, he wondered. How would he communicate with them? David did not know Portuguese, the language of Brazil. Despite this drawback, he decided to ask for food.

His hike brought him to a cottage set in a small clearing. Three dogs darted out and surrounded him. They watched him with cold eyes and barked furiously. He grabbed a stick and kept them at bay.

The man and woman who lived in the cottage called off the dogs. They motioned for him to come inside. David remembered that Latin was the root language for Portuguese. He did know Latin. Sign language and carefully chosen Latin words served him well. He made them understand that he wanted to buy some fresh fruit.

The woman succeeded in setting him down at a table. She made him understand they had nothing ripe except bananas. She instead asked him to share a meal with them. They offered him beef, fish, rice, bananas, bread, cheese, and tapioca.

"Engleese?" the woman asked. "Americano?"

"Engleese," David said. "I am English."

By now the entire family had gathered around to meet the stranger. The children stood along one wall. They looked at him curiously. The woman spoke in rapid Portuguese. Apparently, she was educating her children about the English.

David ate well, intending to pay for the food. The good woman would take none of his money. As David left, she wrapped some food for David to take with him.

As he walked away, the humble cottage looked especially pleasant. The dark forest seemed brighter and less foreboding. David realized that kind hearted people could be found everywhere, even among the peasants in the countryside.

"Rio is great!" David shouted.

As he walked back, he came to a clear stream. It came dashing down from the mountains. David splashed along the creek bed. He sought a waterfall. His efforts were rewarded. Beneath a mountain waterfall, David enjoyed a refreshing shower, his first good bath in seven weeks.

Throughout the voyage, the ship's passengers had longed for a clean bath. Once, when the ship had stopped at sea, David asked the Captain if he could go for a swim in the ocean. The Captain replied silently by pointing to the fin of a great shark. It circled the ship, waiting.

David did not mention the shower to his ship mates until they sailed from Rio. He described the pleasure of standing under the clear water warmed by the tropical sun. The other passengers looked like they would force the Captain to turn back. They wanted to enjoy the waterfall.

"You're a fortunate man," Captain Donaldson said quickly. He addressed David loud enough for everyone to hear. "You risked getting all your clothes stolen. Runaway slaves live in the forest. They frequently rob unsuspecting visitors. I heard last week that a husband and wife were robbed of all they owned."

David wrote home about his experiences in Rio. "You can't imagine with what a light heart I visit these foreign shores. Everything is so different from the idea I formed of them while reading. This is really a fine world we live in after all." At the top of the letter he wrote the date and the ship's position: March 5, 1841 and 35 degrees south latitude, 3 degrees east longitude. That was well out in the South Atlantic on the way to Africa. Unless they met a ship going back to England, the letters would not be posted until he reached Africa. He could expect six months or so from the time he wrote a letter until he received a reply.

They expected to be in Cape Town in a few days. David's thoughts turned to his destination. Cape Town got its name from a hook of land, a cape, at the southern tip of Africa. Sailors had named it as they explored along the coast of Africa for a route to India. The Cape of Good Hope marked the change from the Atlantic Ocean to the Indian Ocean.

The Dutch East India Company had established a trading post in Cape Town. Europeans settled there. Farmers from Holland, called Boers, trekked inland from Cape Town. They had settled where they found good farmland. They did little to explore the country. Their knowledge of Africa ended north of the Orange River where the Kalahari Desert began.

"What do you know about Africa?" David asked Captain Donaldson.

"It's a vast continent," the Captain said. "Africa extends 4000 miles from north to south and 5000 miles from east to west. The Portuguese probably have more ports along Africa's shoreline than anyone else. They seldom travel inland from their trading stations."

David nodded. That agreed with what he had read. The deepest the Portuguese had gone into Africa was but three hundred miles.

Back in his cabin, David unfolded a map of Africa and studied its major features. In northern Africa were the ancient countries of Egypt, Tripoli, Algeria and Morocco. People had lived in northern Africa, especially Egypt, since Old Testament times. Yet, knowledge of Africa ended where those countries met the sands of the Sahara Desert.

Four great rivers flowed out of Africa and into the sea: Nile, Niger, Congo and Zambezi.

The great Nile once hid baby Moses from Pharaoh in the reeds along its bank. The source of this ancient river's headwaters was still a mystery. It disappeared into the desert. Sailing vessels could go no farther than the second set of cataracts near the border of Sudan. Where it began no one knew.

The Niger began in Sierra Leone and made a great curving course to the fabled city of Timbuktu. It then turned south again to empty into the Atlantic below the bulge of Africa. Of Africa's four great rivers, the Niger was the only one that had been explored along its entire route. Even that triumph came at a terrible price. In 1805 Mungo Park began his second safari along the river. He had made 1000 miles before all the Europeans in the expedition, a total of 45 people, perished of disease.

The Congo River flowed west. It drained central Africa and emptied into the Atlantic Ocean. Navigation on it was impossible because of rapids and waterfalls. Its source was unknown.

The Zambezi River was the main river in south central Africa. It flowed east into the Indian Ocean. No one knew where it began. If David pushed north from

Kuruman, he might find its headwaters. His way would be blocked by the Kalahari Desert.

The heart of Africa was held between two deserts—the Sahara and the Kalahari.

No one knew what lay between the Sahara and the Kalahari. People called the middle of Africa the 'heart of darkness' because it was unexplored. Most people thought the Kalahari extended until it met the Sahara. David didn't agree. How could the Nile keep flowing all year long if it drained nothing but desert? Somewhere in that great blank space on his map were grasslands and forests—and a tremendous number of people who'd never heard about Jesus.

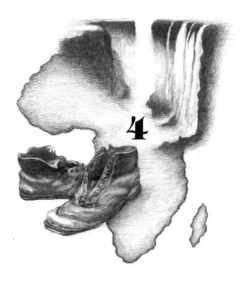

A Prospecting Trip

David Livingstone watched in pleasure and excitement as the scenery of Africa unfolded. He sat on the buckboard of his wagon. Directly ahead of him were the patient oxen, a team of ten animals in five pairs.

A native driver walked alongside of the animals. The oxen plodded ahead at an easy pace. Sometimes one would slow. The driver would flick a rhinoceros whip at the ox that fell behind. He made sure all animals pulled their fair share.

David enjoyed country. The ox wagons trekked through green, grassy meadows lighted by bright African sunshine. Short, scraggy trees broke the flat landscape here and there. Birds sang from the tree branches. Hummingbirds darted about in great numbers. He watched in wonder as they hovered in mid-air, taking nectar from the flowers.

The pace quickened. The animals moved ahead without urging.

David jumped down from the wagon to walk with Pomare. He was a native assistant from Kuruman in charge of the drivers of the oxen. As the son of a chief, he carried himself with a regal bearing.

"The team is moving more quickly," David observed.

"Yes, Doctor Livingstone," Pomare said. "The animals smell water. The Orange River is ahead."

"Where are the elephants?" David asked. "And lions, rhinoceros and zebras?"

Pomare waved forward. "Far ahead, past Kuruman."

"Ouch!" David exclaimed. A small bush seemed to have jumped out and grabbed him. He tried to twist free. Hooked barbs caught his clothes. The more he struggled, the tighter they held. He unbuttoned his shirt. He stepped away and left his shirt behind. Very carefully he freed the shirt from the thorns and put it back on.

Pomare watched all of this with evident delight. He said, "Wait-a-bit."

"Wait-a-bit?" David asked. "Why?"

Pomare said, "Wait-a-bit thorn is the name of that bush."

"It is well named," David agreed. He was learning a lot about Africa since landing at Cape Town.

David had spent a month in Cape Town. Then he had sailed on to Port Elizabeth aboard the *George*. There he outfitted for the long cross-country journey to Kuruman. He bought an ox-wagon, oxen to pull it, and supplies. The wagon cost fifty pounds and the oxen three pounds each. He had spent his first year's salary on wagon, oxen and supplies.

Other people going to Kuruman traveled with him in wagons of their own. The caravan got under way on May 20, 1841. A day's travel averaged ten miles. On sandy ground, or if they crossed rivers or climbed hills, it could be even less.

They approached the river. David climbed back aboard his ox-wagon to buckle everything down firmly. The wagon served as his home on wheels. He had placed the chests that he opened most often near the back. Daily supplies of tea, coffee, rice and flour were at hand. Small lockers along the sides held plates and eating utensils.

Boxes filled the middle of the wagon. He had put a cot on top of them. The cot under the canvas cover of the wagon served as his bed at night. He pitched a tent only when they planned to camp for two or three days in the same place.

The native drivers stopped the wagons at water's edge. The caravan made ready to cross the Orange

River. The driver jumped on the back of one of the oxen next to the wagon. He snapped the whip. The team sloshed into the fast flowing stream. The oxen churned up the silt on the river bottom. One animal turned sideways. It thrashed around.

In an instant, the team had gotten into trouble. It looked as if the oxen would drown or upset the wagon. The team crashed back. The wagon bucked up in front suddenly. David was tossed out. One moment he was holding tightly to the buckboard. The next moment he was standing at the water's edge.

Pomare and two other natives ran to help David and the driver. With a great deal of shouting and arm waving they got the confused animals turned around. They crossed the river and made it safely to the opposite shore.

David looked ahead with excitement and anticipation. He knew that the Orange River marked the end of European control. From here on Africa was wild and mostly unmapped.

"Let's stop for the night," William Ross suggested. He and Mrs. Ross were going to Kuruman, too.

David agreed. "We'll pitch camp and stay an extra night. There's water and grass for the oxen. They need to rest."

"So do we," William Ross said.

The exhausted appearance of his fellow travelers surprised David. His years of toil in the hot cotton mill had given him physical endurance. The wagon trip seemed like a vacation to him.

Everyone jumped into action. Two people went off to gather firewood while the others unyoked the oxen. David started a fire. One of the natives got a bucket and filled it with water from the river. Within thirty minutes they had a hot meal of coffee, biscuits, beans and meat. The meat was wild game, an antelope, taken the previous day.

The natives expected David or one of the other Europeans to supply the meat. David carried a hunting gun and learned how to use it. David only shot for food. He did not understand those who enjoyed killing for sport. David's gun was a primitive weapon, a single-shot muzzle-loader. It had a huge bore and fired a slug three-quarters of an inch across. David learned that the natives were poor shots with a rifle. They did not think in straight lines. A native would point a rifle far too high, expecting the bullet to rise and fall like a spear.

David had begun writing in a journal. He recorded all that he saw and heard. He sketched the streams they crossed, showing their direction and size. He estimated the rise and fall of the landscape. He took compass readings.

"How far have we come?" he wondered. He had attached an odometer to his wagon. This device clicked off each turn of the wheel and converted the wheel's motion to miles. He checked the device. The distance was a disappointing 234 miles. Kuruman lay 300 miles ahead.

David recorded this information in his journal, along with his estimate of their latitude and longitude.

"Mebalwe," David called to one of the natives sitting around the flickering fire. "I have a question for you."

"Yes, Doctor Livingstone," Mebalwe replied. He walked over and sat by David. Mebalwe was a native, a Christian and a trusted worker for the Kuruman missionary station. He was an elderly man, but was very active and dependable.

David said, "In Cape Town I heard stories of a

large fresh water lake far to the north across the Kalahari Desert."

"Yes, I have heard that story, too," Mebalwe said. "Is it true? I do not know."

David said, "If such a lake exists, it may mean the heart of Africa isn't a blazing desert."

"Who can know? Nobody crosses the Kalahari but Bushmen."

Bushmen, David knew, were a hearty stock of nomads who could eke out a living in the most difficult and lifeless terrain. David put away his journal. Someday he would solve the mystery of the lake in the desert.

Mebalwe moved closer. "I am a Christian," he said softly. "I desire to be a preacher of the Gospel to native peoples. I can speak the principle languages and teach them most excellently."

David did not know how to reply. Some missionaries believed native teachers would be the only way to reach all of Africa's people. Other missionaries worried that native teachers were ill-prepared for their duties. Some could not read and many could not write. Those who could write formed letters with painful slowness. As children they never learned the muscle control to shape small letters properly.

Mebalwe tried again. "If you strike out beyond Kuruman, take me with you," he pleaded.

David said, "My orders are to report to Kuruman and wait for direction from Robert Moffat. But . . . yes, when I set out on my own, I'll take you with me."

Satisfied, Mebalwe asked, "Do you enjoy wagon travel?"

"It is quite agreeable. The country is all I expected and more. My only regret is that I can't read or study," David said. "The jarring ride makes it difficult

to hold a book and impossible to read it. It is just as well.
I'm enjoying the countryside too much to read."

After their short stay at the Orange River, the
wagons moved on. They traveled northwest to deliver
supplies to a missionary station at Griqua Town. Then
the route jogged back northeast to Kuruman.

As they neared Kuruman, the country changed. It
became a broad, flat land crossed by dried out riverbeds filled with boulders. Water sometimes flowed in
the rivers. The thin stream would soak into the sun
baked soil. Baobab trees waited for the rains. Their
spindly limbs stayed bare of leaves until the rains came.
Then the leaves would bud. The huge trunks would
become water tanks, storing water for the dry season.

Despite the hardships, life found a way to flourish
in the parched soil. David saw spiders, scorpions, ants,
lizards and frogs. The frogs, called matlametlo, fascinated him. In the heat of summer a matlametlo would
dig a hole deep in the ground under a bush. There it
waited patiently for the wet season. Often a spider
would spin a web across the opening. It was as if the
frog had a screen door over his hole.

Finally, David arrived at Kuruman on July 31,
1841. The trek from Port Elizabeth had covered 530
miles. They had gained a half mile in elevation as they
climbed into Africa's highlands. The trip, including
detours to visit two missionary stations, took 72 days.

The missionary settlement at Kuruman was a
pleasant oasis. Robert Moffat had been a gardener
before becoming a missionary. At Kuruman he had
planted orchards and gardens. He also built an impressive stone church. The building looked as if it had been
picked up in England and dropped into the African
countryside. The building was far larger than David
had imagined it would be.

The Sunday services were well attended by 350 natives. Only about 40 were Christians. The nonbelievers came and listened politely out of respect for the Moffats and the other missionaries who labored at Kuruman.

David lodged with Rogers Edwards and his wife. He was a man in his forties. Rogers had lived in Kuruman for almost as long as the Moffats. Rogers longed to move away from Kuruman and build a missionary station of his own. Rogers said, "I've labored here all of these years, yet until now I've not been allowed to move on to a new field."

David listened with growing alarm. Suppose his assignment kept him at Kuruman for years. David said, "Kuruman makes me feel vaguely uneasy. This place feels too settled, too civilized, too comfortable."

"Robert Moffat will kick it into action when he returns," Rogers said.

David said, "My estimate is the total population within a day's travel of here is less than a thousand. The number of missionaries is too large." As he named them, he ticked them off with his fingers: "There's myself, you and your wife, William Ross and his wife, the two native teachers Mebalwe and Paul, and Robert Moffat and his wife."

Rogers said, "An older missionary named Hamilton will return from Griqua Town soon. And Robert Moffat will bring two recruits with him. Yes, Kuruman has its share of missionaries. I have finally received permission from the society directors to search for a suitable site for a new station. Would you like to accompany me?"

"Yes, but . . . my orders are to stay at Kuruman and receive direction from Robert Moffat. I should wait here for his return."

"You could wait months," Rogers said. "The Moffat family is still in England. Printing the New Testament in Sichuana is taking longer than he expected."

David immediately decided to go with Rogers Edwards. The two missionaries huddled together to plan the expedition. It would be a prospecting trip, but not for gold. David and Rogers would look for a suitable place for a missionary outpost.

Rogers Edwards said, "I think a small expedition would be best."

David agreed. He thought small would mean three or four people besides themselves to help with the oxen.

Rogers idea of small was vastly different. He said, "We'll need three wagons, forty oxen, twelve native drivers, and a few assistants. I'd like to take Pomare and Sehamy." Sehamy was a youth, friendly and eager to please. He spoke no English and was not a Christian.

David remembered the plea from the elderly native teacher. David asked, "What about Mebalwe?"

"Yes, he is a good choice, too," Rogers agreed. "Mebalwe is a good handyman."

"Why do the natives have a reputation for being so dull?" David wondered aloud to Rogers.

Rogers said, "A chief would be upset if one of his people revealed information that might help a rival tribe. So they often pretend to be ignorant until they know they can trust you. Then you learn that they are far brighter than they first appeared."

David agreed with that opinion. "Their knowledge of livestock and the best pasture for them is first rate. They know where to plant gardens and fields for growing grain. Their understanding of wild animals is remarkably accurate."

The expedition left Kuruman. As the miles rolled away, the countryside grew less severe. Grasses, brush and a few trees grew. Creeping vines sent out runners underfoot. David was surprised to see wild cucumbers, gourds and watermelons. Herds of animals feasted on the grass and vines: antelopes, springboks, impalas and zebra. He saw ostriches, ocelots, and an occasional jackal.

"Native tribes should be attracted to the plentiful game in this area," David said. But he also knew the climate was changing. They had crossed dry riverbeds which once had flowed with water year-round.

Pomare called, "Elephant!"

Finally, David saw elephants in the wild. He raced forward to watch the herd. They were busy knocking down trees and eating them. The herd moved on and was soon out of sight.

David walked forward to see where the elephants had foraged. He measured the branch against his thumb. "Look at this," he told Rogers. "The branches are as thick as my thumb with thorns an inch long. Yet the elephants ate them as if they were tender shoots of grass. They must have a marvelous digestive system."

They entered lion country. One day six lions stood within 20 yards of the wagons. The caravan rolled cautiously forward. The lions switched their tails, turned slowly and walked out of their way.

That night a roar awoke David. Sehamy ran to his side. "*Simba!*" he cried.

Lions! David grabbed his rifle. A distressed cry came from the oxen. Natives threw more wood on the fire. The flames flared up and cast flickering light around the camp. A rumble, a sound made deep in a lion's throat, came from the darkness. Light reflected from the lions' eyes as they paced outside the circle of flames. Then the lions left the camp.

The next morning, David found the extent of the attack. One of the oxen had been killed and carried away. The expedition took its toll on the oxen. Two fell into pitfalls dug by natives to take game. One died of natural causes.

Their route took them to Chonuane, a village of the Bakwena tribe. The name Bakwena meant "People of the Crocodile." Sechele was their chief. David learned that the chief's son was sick with dysentery. He began a series of treatments that cured the boy. Chief Sechele opened his village to them.

He agreed to let David talk to the village about Jesus. For the first time, David held a public worship service for the Africans. Mebalwe translated as David spoke. In the sermon David mentioned the final judgment before the great throne of God. He described the place prepared for those who loved God, and the place for the evil ones.

After the service, Chief Sechele said, "It is the custom to question any new subject brought to me. Will you answer questions?"

David agreed.

Chief Sechele said, "Did your forefathers know of a future judgment?"

David replied, "Yes. This is nothing new. It has been in Scripture since the beginning."

"You startle me," Chief Sechele said. "What you describe makes my bones to shake. My forefathers were living at the same time as your forefathers. How is it that they did not receive word about these things sooner? They passed away into darkness without knowing whither they were going."

David drew back, astonished. He was not dealing with an ordinary individual. Chief Sechele showed unusual intelligence. David stammered an explanation, "The way has been difficult. Great barriers prevented my forefathers from traveling into Africa."

Chief Sechele said, "Must the tribes beyond the Kalahari forever remain ignorant of Christianity?"

Surprised, David asked, "You know of tribes on the other side of the Kalahari?"

"Yes, they are led by the great chief Sebituane. I, Sechele of the Bakwena have visited them."

"When?" David asked.

"Before the land grew dry you could cross the Kalahari during the wet season. Watermelons and cucumbers grew. Wells could be dug down to water. Now it is impossible."

Later David asked Rogers Edwards about Chief Sechele. "Do you think he has crossed the Kalahari?" David asked.

Rogers said, "It is difficult to know for sure. When a person becomes chief, he inherits the heroic deeds of his father and grandfather. It is possible his father, grandfather, or even great-grandfather did cross the Kalahari. In their way of speech, he is not lying when he says he did it."

David wasn't so much interested in *who* did it. He wanted to know that it could be done.

After leaving Chief Sechele, they continued northeast. They skirted the southern fringes of the desert. They traveled for ten days across the dreary wilderness without seeing another individual. Game disappeared. The previous night they had boiled the last of their meat. It was an old and tough piece of rhinoceros. Tonight they would make a porridge of Indian cornmeal and broth from the last of the meat. After that—

"Look," David said, "There is movement in the brush." He unclipped his heavy rifle.

David and Rogers left the others and crept closer.

"It's a Bushman," David said. The wiry little desert dweller worked around a small fire. The Bushman was grinding the stems of a plant. He squeezed the juice into a small pot before him. He finished by swirling the tips of his arrows in the mixture.

"His arrows are poison tipped," Rogers Edwards said.

David nodded. He stood and walked confidently toward the Bushman. The Bushman appeared to ignore them. But he knew they were there. Probably he had seen them before they had seen him. The Bushman stood to his full height of less than five feet. He made no effort to flee. Neither did he appear to welcome the visitors.

Communicating with the Bushman was especially frustrating. He spoke a language far removed from Sechuana. Many of the words contained a clicking sound made with the tongue.

David made the universal sign for food—hand pointing into the mouth. The Bushman smiled broadly and pointed ahead. David scanned the horizon and detected a faint smudge of smoke.

"Ah! There is a village," David said. "We can be there by tomorrow afternoon."

The Bushman had gathered his few possessions and wandered away.

At every opportunity David collected samples for the scientists back home. His most recent discovery was pieces of petrified trees to send to Professor Owen. David could not pass up the scientific mystery of the poison arrows. He crushed the plant the Bushman had used and made a juice of it. He touched the juice to the outside of his lips. They became numb. His tongue burned and the smell was very sharp. He mixed in some vinegar. The mixture became bland and harmless. "This proves the poison is a type of chemical known as an alkali," David told Rogers.

The next day they drew near the village. It was a large one in a valley between two mountains. David and Rogers entered the village. It was deserted and quiet except for the village elders. They stood in a semicircle behind the chief.

"What do you see?" Rogers asked.

David looked around casually. "I see a nearly empty village with the chief and his elders waiting outside the council house for our approach. What do you see?"

Rogers said, "It's what I don't see. I can imagine hundreds of warriors lurking out of sight. They're grasping spears and axes. They await the signal from the suspicious chief. In a flash they will dart out and hack us to death."

David stopped the procession at the center of the village. "We'll make camp here," he decided.

Rogers whispered, "A story is told about a village like this in these mountains. The villagers were guilty of a terrible crime. A white man and his company came peacefully to the village to trade. The villagers gave the trader food and water. It was poisoned. They killed him and all those with him. They ate his oxen and plundered his trading goods. They even pried the iron from his wagon and broke up the wood for their fires."

David asked, "Is this that village?"

"Probably not," Rogers said. But he did not sound too confident.

The party started a fire, put on a kettle of water, and pitched out their bed rolls. David lay down and calmly took a nap.

The Rainmaker

David Livingstone awoke to find the entire village had surrounded them. The children poked their heads between the legs of the circle of adults. They reached out and touched David's long, straight hair. The women seemed fascinated by David's appearance. A woman reached out and touched his nose. The natives laughed, amazed that it was real.

David said, "They must think ours are too long to be real, compared to their own button size noses."

The chief welcomed the travelers. He introduced himself. "I am Moseealele, Chief of the Bakhatla." He gave them milk, porridge, boiled beans and deer meat. He gave David and Rogers each an ostrich egg and tiger's skin. Rogers completed the custom of a formal gift exchange by giving to the chief some beads, cloth and sewing needles. The chief seemed entirely satisfied with the exchange.

David saw that the chief suffered from an eye infection, which he offered to treat. Chief Moseealele became excited when he learned that David was a doctor. He motioned for David to follow. They walked toward one of the small huts placed near the chief's large house.

Rogers said, "This is the home of his favorite wife."

The chief took David inside. He took his wife's hand and held it out for David to see. A large tumor, red and uncomfortable, made the hand nearly useless. The chief looked at David. His eyes begged for David to help her.

David nodded, "Yes, I can cut the growth off. It will be painful." Doctors for centuries had tried to find ways to help their patient during an operation. So far they had no dependable way to deaden the pain.

Pomare translated, telling the woman what to expect. She took a deep breath and nodded. She pulled a robe around her face. Rogers, who could not stand watching surgery, excused himself and stepped outside.

David began the operation. He made a series of incisions. He cut deep enough to get the root of the growth so it wouldn't return. After removing the growth, he stitched the cuts and bandaged the hand. The brave woman had not even flinched during the entire procedure.

"You are a real heroine," David said and touched the woman gently.

She looked up with a smile.

The tribe lived in a fertile valley between mountain ranges. The mountains looked large compared to the flat wilderness through which they had traveled. The village enjoyed a plentiful supply of pure water. It flowed from a spring at the base of the mountain. Trees, gardens, and fields of grain grew along the stream before it soaked into the ground.

David and Rogers decided to spend a few days with the Bakhatla. Many of the natives had never seen white people. David could not take off his shirt because villagers would encircle him, amazed at the sight of white skin. David unpacked his shaving kit. One of the young village children showed curiosity about the mirror. David let him hold the looking glass. The young boy went into spasms of laughter at his own image.

David noticed that his compass gave an inaccurate reading. He discovered that the mountains were the cause. The mountains contained iron ore that pulled the compass needle off course.

The villagers extracted the iron ore, refined it, and made iron picks, axes and spear-tips. By now the villagers looked upon David as an honored guest. They offered to let him see the ore smelter, a process they had never allowed an outsider to observe. The furnace was a dome shaped chamber made of clay. They dropped ore in the top upon a fuel of charcoal. At the bottom men made a blast of air from leather bellows. When the ore got hot enough, iron flowed out.

What David saw looked familiar. In a book he had seen drawings of how the ancient Egyptians refined iron. It showed men sitting cross legged and blowing air into a clay furnace much like this one. The Egyptians in the time of the pharaohs must have used a process very similar to this one. Had these people learned the secret centuries ago from travelers who came from Egypt?

David understood the chemical process of iron smelting. Carbon must be combined with oxygen in the ore. This frees the iron, which becomes molten and flows out of the bottom of the smelter. The Bakhatla let the charcoal fuel serve as a source of carbon. David knew they could extract more iron by adding another source of carbon, such as limestone.

He found a sample of limestone, which was plentiful in the area. He suggested they mix the rock with the iron ore.

"Does limestone also contain iron?" the smelter workers asked.

David gave his answer. "No, but it will help free the iron."

The workers talked among themselves.

"What are they saying?" David asked.

Pomare answered, "They cannot see the usefulness of putting in with the ore another stone in which there is no iron."

The Bakhatla ignored his advice. David had seen this before. He would speak to them about the Good News of Jesus. The natives would listen with great respect. Yet, when he finished, they would ignore what he had said. On this trip, only Chief Sechele had seemed moved by the Gospel message. All others gave him their utmost attention—and then walked away as if he had not addressed them.

The visit with the Bakhatla was the last major stop on their trip. When they returned to Kuruman, David plotted their route on a map of Africa. The circuit took three months and covered 700 miles. At their farthest point, they were 200 miles north of Kuruman. David was surprised to learn that he had already gone farther north than any other missionary. Yet, their expedition was but a tiny circuit on the face of the Dark Continent. How could missionaries hope to cover so vast a country?

He learned that the Moffat family had arrived safely in Port Elizabeth. However, they had become separated from their baggage, which had been sent on a separate ship. The ship with their luggage had not yet been seen. The Moffats would be delayed for weeks while they collected their belongings.

"What to do?" David wondered aloud one evening while studying in Rogers Edwards' home. They had been back from their trip for three months. Rogers Edwards had written to the London Missionary Society directors for permission to start a new mission station. Their reply had not yet come.

Rogers said, "When Robert Moffat gets underway, his progress will be slow. He will stop often to meet and confer with missionaries along the way."

"Would I have time to go out alone?" David asked.

"Whatever for?" Rogers asked.

David explained, "I've been mobbed by natives seeking medical aid. Yesterday, they surrounded me so thoroughly I could not walk outside. They travel from a hundred miles away. They come to me, although their own medicine men could treat most cases. By leaving I would lighten the press of medical work."

"Is that the only reason for leaving?" Rogers Edwards asked.

"No," David admitted. "I find it difficult at Kuruman to learn the native language and customs. By moving away I'll acquire fluency in Sichuan and preach directly to the natives."

"You'll have time," Rogers assured him.

On February 10, 1842 David set out with only one wagon and four people. He took the two native teachers Paul and Mebalwe and two men to manage the wagon. He decided upon Lepelole as his destination. Chief Bubi, the leader there, had welcomed them on his first tour.

In the villages David talked to the natives. He learned as much as he could about the countryside. He found the medicine men, who often also served as rainmakers, to have a surprisingly useful knowledge of the local herbs that could cure minor disorders.

At Lepelole he found the medicine man sitting outside his hut surrounded by pots filled with medicines.

"Hail, friend!" David called to the man. "I see you are surrounded by medicines. What is the purpose of so many medicines?"

The rain man said, "The whole country needs the rain I am making."

David asked, "Do you really believe you can command the clouds? I think that is done by God alone."

The rain man said, "If we have no rain, the cattle would have no pasture, the cows give no milk, our children become lean and die, our wives run away to other tribes who do make rain and have corn."

David said, "I quite agree with you as to the value of the rain. But you cannot charm the clouds by medicines."

The rain man looked at David. "When a patient dies, you don't give up trust in your medicines; neither do I when rain fails."

David said, "God alone can command the clouds. God will give us rain without your medicines." David had tried time and again to convince the people of the false belief in charms. Their faith in medical charms seemed unlimited.

The medicine man said, "I suppose you can make rain."

David said, "Yes. A stream flows nearby. By

hard work we can dig a canal and bring the water to the village crops."

David examined the slope of the land. The water canal would need to be three feet wide, four feet deep and four or five hundred feet long. Several people working a few hours every day for a few weeks could provide a never ending supply of "rain."

When Chief Bubi heard about David's plan, he was all for it. Chief Bubi promised, "I will give you as many men as you need."

The only drawback was the lack of proper tools. David found only one spade. It had a broken handle. Mebalwe, who was good with his hands, said, "We will make do. We can use tortoise shells as scoops and baskets to carry away the dirt."

When the rainmaker saw David's intentions, he joined in the work. "The foreigner is very cunning to make rain so," he said.

This was one of David Livingstone's great characteristics. He showed respect to the chiefs and medicine men, and thus won their trust. He could make even those who would normally be his enemies like him. He also made certain that they respected him. He would not tell them to do something that he was not willing to do himself. He worked along side the villagers in digging the canal. The work exposed him to the sun during the middle of the day and he suffered sunburn on both legs and arms.

One day some visitors from another village watched the digging. They spoke to the workers. "Missionaries in our village pay us for such work," the visitors said.

The next morning, David's crew assembled at the work site. They refused to take up their buckets and baskets. They said, "We ought to be paid for our work."

David said, "It is my kindness to show you how to do this work. Instead of me paying you, I am the one who should be paid."

The workers repeated what they had heard from the travelers. "It is only our due," they said. "If other missionaries do it, then you should pay us, too."

David put down the shovel. "If you are unhappy, I shall stop instantly and go to another village." He left the work and walked purposely toward his wagon. "Paul, Mebalwe, come! Pack the wagon. We are no longer welcome here."

Chief Bubi ran to his side. "You must not think of leaving us. It was our foolishness speaking."

The natives had gathered their tools and now stood around David, begging his return. "Yes!" they cried. "We are sorry we spoke so. Do not cease to show us how to work."

David did not spend all of his time at Lepelole. After they finished the water course, he decided to explore. It was now the dry season. The grasses had turned brown, the gourds dried up and the watermelons shriveled. The landscape became parched and sandy.

Mebalwe said, "The oxen are sick and the sand is deep. They will not be able to pull the wagon."

David said, "Let the animals rest. You take them back to Kuruman when they recover. I will go ahead on foot."

As he set out, two young Africans joined the party, Sehamy and Baba. Neither one could speak English. They did not know that David understood their native tongue. He overheard the two boys talking.

"He is not strong," Sehamy said.

"His legs are powerful," Baba replied.

Sehamy didn't agree. "No. He is quite slim. He only appears to have strong legs because he puts himself into those trousers. He will soon fall from exhaustion."

David understood that they were discussing his appearance and strength. He began to walk faster. He kept a fast pace for mile after mile. The next morning, he awoke early and got the party underway. For three days he maintained a blistering pace.

Finally, Sehamy cried, "*Bwana*, rest."

As he passed through the desert, David continued to write in his journal. He learned knowledge of the countryside. He took note of 32 roots that could be eaten and 43 fruits that grew wild.

One day as they walked along, a little bird flew over their heads. It chirped as if trying to get their attention.

Sehamy said, "That is the honey guide. It will take us to honey."

David thought at first he might be joking. But the bird flew around their heads and chirped, calling for them to follow. David and Sehamy set out in the direction the bird flew. It waited on a tree limb and chirped insistently. Then it flew ahead impatiently. The tree with the honey was more than four miles away. Sehamy made a fire and smoked the hive, pulling out the rich and sweet honey comb of the wild honeybees. He left some of the wax and larvae for the honey bird.

He prepared a meal of locusts and wild honey. After roasting the locusts, he pounded and mixed them with honey.

David sampled Sehamy's creation. "It tastes like shrimp," David said.

"You like it?" Sehamy asked.

"Many people think shrimp is a great delicacy," David assured the boy. He did not add that he had never liked shrimp. But in the desert, locusts and wild honey could be a welcome change.

Once again David returned to Kuruman. He learned that Robert Moffat and his caravan had not even left Cape Town.

David talked with Rogers Edwards. "More than two years ago I first set foot in Africa. The directors have given me permission to move forward. Yet, I hesitate because they assumed Robert Moffat would be here to give me specific direction. Should I wait for his return?"

He talked not only with Rogers Edwards, but with other missionaries at Kuruman. "The hot weather will begin in October," Hamilton, the old man, said. "You need to construct your chapel and a place to live before then or wait until next season. You will need help in constructing a missionary station. Rogers Edwards would be the perfect choice. He is skilled with tools, so he will be a great help in putting up a chapel."

David decided to go out again.

Rogers Edwards agreed to go with David to help build the new missionary station.

"Where should we go?" David wondered. "Drought and warfare between rival parties has destroyed Lepelole. Chief Bubi and his people have moved on."

Rogers said, "I recommend Mabotsa. It is 220 miles north east of Kuruman."

David remembered going through it with Rogers on their first circuit. "You're right. It is well suited for a mission station. The weather is good and there is water. Even trees grow there."

Moselele, the chief of Mabotsa, welcomed the

two missionaries. He offered them land for free. David
and Rogers believed it best to purchase the land out-
right. They drew up a deed. They paid for the land with
a hunting rifle, some powder, lead shot and beads. The
first building would be a chapel measuring 18 by 50
feet. It would be the biggest building in the village.

David did not just visit Mabotsa. He moved there.
Would Robert Moffat look upon this with favor? Or,
would he charge that David had disobeyed orders?
Would he write the directors and tell them that David
was unfit for the mission field?

Well, David decided, *if they withdraw their support, I will set out on my own. That was my original
plan anyway.* But he knew his efforts would be much
easier with Robert Moffat on his side.

Making an impression on the unbelieving natives
was far more difficult than David had imagined. They
looked upon the Europeans in wonder and delight.
They welcomed them to their village. But the Gospel—
no, it was not for them.

Communicating in a foreign language was a
problem. Missionaries used a Sichuana word for
"holy." David learned the word meant "a nice fat ox"
to the Mabotsa. The natives had no word at all for
"soul." The closest word was one meaning "breath."
Some of the hymns they sang had a phrase such as
"anchored in Jesus." But the natives had never seen a
large body of water. They had never seen an anchor nor
did they know its purpose.

Puzzling conversations often took place when
words sounded alike. David noticed that the phrase
"thank you" (*kia itumela*) sounded a lot like the
phrase "I am lost" (*kia timela*). The word for "water"
(*metse*) could be confused with the phrase "I have
been lost" (*ki timetse*).

The European explorer may say to the native, "Take us to the wagons."

The native may reply, "I am lost. I have been lost."

The explorer may think the native said "Thank you. I want water." So the explorer replies, "Take us to the wagon and we will give you water."

The native is confused now. He repeats again that he is lost.

The explorer is just as confused. He goes into greater detail insisting the native show them the way and they will give him water. The native continues to repeat that he is lost. In the end the explorer concludes that the native is addled or intentionally playing stupid.

David had been in Africa for two years. As far as he knew, not a single person had become a believer in Jesus because of his efforts. Sometimes he felt very lonely. Even his friend Mebalwe and Rogers Edwards and his wife, could not relieve the loneliness pressing upon David. Mail had not come from home.

He wrote home, "Next month I expect to receive letters from home. What are you all doing? I hear no answer but the still, deathlike quietness in this wilderness land. Here in the evenings I hear the bleating of sheep and goats, the lowing of oxen. The jabber of the natives mingles with the yell of the jackal and howling of the wolf. Occasionally the natives dance and screech their own wild unearthly music the greater portion of the night. I have written very often to you, but I don't get letters from you."

In November, 1843 David received word that Robert Moffat had arrived at Kuruman. David was so lonely, he welcomed the news. He left immediately to meet him. It would be best for Robert Moffat to hear about the new missionary station straight from David.

6

The Eyes of Death

David made his way to Kuruman. The caravan carrying Moffat still had not arrived. David was told, "He is still south of Kuruman, making slow progress from Cape Town." Quickly, David saddled a horse and set off to meet Robert Moffat.

Four days out from Kuruman, David paused on a hillside overlooking the Vaal River valley. Far off in the distance he saw a smudge of dust. Only travelers with several wagons and a large number of oxen would churn up such a cloud of dust.

Suddenly, David was seized with great excitement. In the valley below was Robert Moffat, the world's best known missionary to Africa. David urged the horse into action, racing across the valley in a headlong gallop. He reined up next to Robert Moffat's wagon. The caravan stopped. David jumped from his horse and Robert Moffat stepped down from the wagon.

The two men embraced. David could not contain his excitement.

The commanding physical presence and impressive stature of the man again struck David. Robert Moffat was 48 years old. He stood more than six feet tall. He had a long black beard streaked with gray. He had sharp clear eyes.

David tied his reins to the wagon and rode back to Kuruman with Robert Moffat. All along the way they exchanged the latest news. Robert Moffat told about what was happening in the rest of the world. David described his adventures in Africa.

They began talking at noon and continued to talk until the caravan stopped for the night. David helped make camp. He enjoyed the end of day devotion and joined the voices singing evening hymns. They all fell silent to watch the spectacular sunset over the rolling grassy plains.

After everyone else had gone to bed, David and Robert continued to talk by the light of the camp fire. David brought up the subject of the missionary outpost at Mabotsa.

Robert Moffat gave his blessing to the endeavor. He said, "I believe firmly in pushing further inland."

David also cautiously opened the subject of native assistants.

Robert Moffat understood exactly the question. "Do we build a large missionary station and staff it with the best missionaries who have been carefully trained? Or, do we scatter throughout the countryside small missionary posts staffed by an African assistant who may be enthusiastic but ill equipped? I do not think the time is right for such a step."

David said, "Mebalwe has proven to be a valuable assistant."

Robert Moffat said, "He is an exceptional individual. We have few others like him. The next generation of natives will be better educated and more thoroughly trained."

Robert Moffat held out a bound book. "This will be a start," he said. "I have spent decades with this goal—a New Testament in the language of the African people. I've ordered a printing press. At Kuruman we'll print the new Bible and other religious books. Kuruman will have a school to teach the natives to read and write in their own language. Someday, native teachers will be entirely able to teach the Gospel."

All of David's fears about Robert Moffat vanished. Their love for the mission field overcame any disagreement.

Kuruman came to life when Robert Moffat returned. Soon the settlement bustled with new energy. David enjoyed being with the Moffat family. He stayed with them much longer than he had intended. After an enjoyable Christmas at Kuruman, he traveled back to Mabotsa. He arrived there on January 2, 1844.

His duties, such as collecting scientific specimens and treating the sick, took him outside the village. Sometimes David would not be back until after dark. Chief Moselele worried about such trips. The chief said, "When you go beyond the village, even for a short distance, I will send an attendant to be with you."

Rogers Edwards explained, "They have good grounds for their fears. Lions are a real problem."

David agreed. It was the dry season and hot. In the southern hemisphere, the seasons are reversed from the northern hemisphere. December, January and February were the summer months in Mabotsa. Game disappeared to better grazing grounds. Desperate lions raided the villages. Lions found the livestock of the villagers to be easy prey. The animals were in pens and could not escape. At first the lions came at night. They leaped into the cattle pens and carried away the cows. The lions became more bold. They attacked herds during the day.

Tragedy struck while David was at Mabotsa. A lion attacked and killed a woman as she worked in her garden near the town. Her children could not be consoled. Their bitter cries could be heard throughout the village.

"We are bewitched," the villagers cried to David.

"Nonsense," he told them.

The villagers said, "Lions do not attack in the day. A neighboring tribe has bewitched us and given us over to the lions."

David said, "You know the remedy. Kill one of the lions and the others will stay away."

"We are afraid," the villagers said. "You do it for us."

David said, "You are entirely capable of protecting yourselves."

They disagreed. "We have twice hunted them but returned without killing any."

David knew what had actually happened. Fifty of the villagers had surrounded a pride of lions. When the animals roared, the hunters ran away in fear. They were quite convinced that they had been bewitched. They had lost their courage.

David said, "The next time I will come with you to give you courage. But you must kill the lion."

David had learned the advantage of digging a canal to irrigate the fields at Lepelole. He had shared this success with Chief Moselele. With the chief's support David and a team of volunteers began digging a canal at Mabotsa.

On February 16, 1844 an excited villager interrupted the work on the water course. He rushed up
breathlessly. "Lions have just dragged off some
sheep!" he announced. "Hunters are going to track
them down."

David decided to go with the hunting party, more
to encourage the hunters than to do the job himself.

They found the lions on a small hill. David could
see, now and then, some of the lions moving around.
The lions hid among the trees. The men, armed with
spears, encircled the hill. They walked up the hill,
keeping one another in sight. They closed the circle
around the lions.

David and Mebalwe waited below the hill. David
was armed with a double barrel rifle. Mebalwe had an
ancient flintlock.

Some of the lions retreated into the center of the
circle. Others broke through the circle.

"Why didn't they spear him?" Mebalwe asked.
"They were close enough."

David said, "The men are afraid to attack him.
They still believe in witchcraft."

A lion stood on an exposed ledge of rock. Silently
Mebalwe raised his rife. He fired. The bullet missed its
mark. It struck the rock at the lion's feet. The lion
slapped at the spot with his paw, as if brushing aside an
annoying insect. The lion jumped down and broke
through the circle of hunters.

"They let him get away, too," David observed.
He decided he would have to help them kill one of the
lions. The woman who had been killed by a lion was
still a strong memory.

The circle reformed around two of the big cats.
The men were too close together for David to get a
clean shot. The men shouted. The lions burst through

the circle on the other side. The hunting party closed the circle and met at the top of the hill.

"All have escaped," David observed. "Let's go back to the village."

As they walked around the hill, David glimpsed one of the big cats sitting behind a cover of brush. David took aim. He fired with both barrels.

It looked as if the lion fell. The brush hid his body. One of the natives cried, "He is shot! He is shot!"

"Let us get him!" the natives now cried. They rushed down the hill toward the lion.

David saw the lion's tail standing straight up above the brush. A lion held its tail that way when angry. Mebalwe walked toward the lion.

"Stop," David warned. "Wait until I reload."

As David rammed down the bullet, he heard a warning shout.

David turned half way around. The lion sprang and landed on David. Powerful jaws clamped his left shoulder. Sharp teeth crunched through his thick tartan jacket, his shirt, skin, muscles and bones. The lion growled. He shook David as easily as a dog shakes a rat.

David felt himself becoming warm and uncaring. All fear left him. The shock produced a stupor. He was entirely conscious but could neither resist nor feel pain.

The lion had a paw on the back of his head. He shifted around and saw the lion's eyes—the eyes of death. The lion looked away. Someone had distracted the lion. Had the villagers come to his rescue? No, they were too far away. It was Mebalwe.

Mebalwe was thirty feet away. He lifted his weapon. It was an ancient flintlock, prone to misfire. The lion let go of David. It charged Mebalwe.

The brave man stood his ground. He fired one

barrel. It misfired. He pulled the other trigger. It failed to fire, too. The lion tore into Mebalwe's thigh. The lion's powerful jaws tore through flesh, cutting all the way to the bone.

Baba now joined the fight. The young man rushed forward and tried to spear the enraged lion. The lion whirled and caught Baba by the shoulder. The lion ripped open his shoulder.

Suddenly the lion released Baba. As quickly as the attack began, it ended. The lion died. David's original shots had struck the animal. Now the bullets took effect and brought down the great beast.

As the shock wore off David, the pain returned. The damage to David's shoulder was terrible. The lion had crushed the bones to splinters. The lion's teeth left eleven punctures as deep as knife wounds.

The natives carried the three victims to the village. They put David in one of their huts. Gently they rested him on a mat. They sheltered him from the sun and treated his wounds.

David awoke the next morning. He couldn't move. The pain was so sharp it left him breathless. Fever raged. Chief Moselele ordered the best care. The villagers worked in relays, not allowing him to be alone.

Despite the terrible attack, Chief Moselele's people rejoiced. They danced around the dead lion. They assured David it was one of the largest they had ever seen. The villagers believed fire purged a charm. The next day they built a huge bonfire over the lion's carcass.

After a week, David could get up, but only with helping hands. Three weeks passed. David recovered movement in his legs and right arm. The left arm couldn't be used. It had become inflamed, raw, and the wounds oozed an unpleasant discharge. The arm itself was hot to the touch.

One night as the fever raged he dreamed he was in London. He rested between clean sheets in a cool hospital room. Dr. Bennet came in and dressed his arm properly. Then Dr. Bennet sat on the edge of the bed. They talked as good friends do, sharing their hopes and plans for the future.

He awoke the next morning. David nearly cried when he realized it had been a dream.

David was the only doctor around, so he had to give advice to the village medicine man and oversee his own treatment. As he moved the left arm, he could see the bones moving around. The joint was shattered. "The joint must be rebuilt," he told Rogers Edwards. "Otherwise, I'll never be able to use the arm again."

"But how?" Rogers asked. He'd done his best to help David recover, but he was no doctor. He couldn't stand the sight of the mangled shoulder.

David flexed his left shoulder. A knob moved under the skin as he moved the arm. "See. That is a loose bone. It is out of place and protrudes against the flesh. It needs to be reset."

Rogers Edwards looked at David as if his injured friend had taken leave of his senses. He cried, "You intend to reset it yourself! Impossible! I'll have nothing to do with it. You'll pass out from the pain."

David said, "I have a high tolerance for pain."

Rogers Edwards was shaking his head. "I simply will have no part of this. You might stay conscious throughout, but I wouldn't."

David relied on a couple of trusted villagers to reset the bone. He would need another few weeks of care while he recovered.

He told Chief Moselele, "It would be unfair to

continue to depend upon your generosity. I'll return to Kuruman to recover."

His admiration for Kuruman had grown during his four years in Africa. Now that he understood the importance of water, he saw why Robert Moffat had chosen this place. It had a never failing supply of water from a series of springs in a cave. Robert Moffat had dug a watercourse that branched to bring water to all the buildings. The spring water caused the desert to bloom. In an orchard grew peach, apricot, apple, almond and pear trees. The orchard provided a shady and cool place to walk and talk in the heat of the afternoon.

He walked through the orchard with Mary Moffat, the older daughter of the Moffat family. She had appointed herself David's nurse. She changed the bandages, cooked for him, and insisted on being with him. He enjoyed Mary's company.

In Scotland, David had read books by brave travelers who explored Africa. They described their deeds in heroic terms. Yet, this courageous young woman with him had seen more adventure in her life than most explorers. She had been born in Africa and grew up in the dangerous country. Yet, she thought nothing of her adventures. Instead, she merely wanted to do the will of God and serve Him.

David said, "Your father has done a remarkable job here."

Mary nodded. "At first he became discouraged. The Gospel was slow to take root in African hearts. Father tells me that eight years passed before he had his first convert."

David strolled thoughtfully beside her. He confessed, "I have yet to make a single believer."

She reminded him of what the Bible said. "Sometimes one person does the planting, another the watering, but Jesus gives the increase."

As they enjoyed the pleasant gardens, David was surprised at the things he told her. He had been needing someone with whom to share his life. They sat down on a bench together.

She asked, "What passed through your mind when the lion attacked?"

David laughed. "I wondered what part of me he would eat first. The lion's violent shaking produced a dreaminess. All sense of pain or terror left me, although I was quite conscious of all that was happening. The shake seems to be like the stupor caused when a cat shakes a mouse."

Mary sat by him, fascinated by his story.

Thoughtfully, David said, "This peculiar state is probably produced by all animals that kill their prey. If so, it is a merciful provision by our Creator for lessening the pain of death."

Mary smiled. "You describe the event with the detachment of a scientist," she said.

David said, "I've hardly mentioned the attack in my letters home. I don't want to worry my family. To my other friends, I don't want to publicize my behavior. I unwisely involved myself in the village's affairs. I should have gone better armed and showed greater caution."

Mary examined the arm. She said, "It is a terrible wound."

David said, "Despite the deep cuts and broken bones, infection was not severe. I was wearing a Tartan jacket. I believe that it wiped virus from the teeth that pierced the flesh. Mebalwe and Baba have suffered a great deal of discharge from their wounds."

"How are they?" Mary asked.

"They both will recover. Baba is almost well. Mebalwe heals more slowly."

"Will your arm be all right?" Mary asked.

"Not entirely. I can't lift my left arm higher than my shoulder. It isn't very strong when extended. I'll have to learn to shoot with the rifle barrel braced against a tree. Or, maybe I can switch shoulders and shoot supporting the gun barrel with my right hand."

Despite being so far removed from civilization, Mary was well read and well schooled. Her mother had seen to her education. Mary learned all the skills of making a life in primitive surroundings. She could sew, cook, make candles, and was an expert in household matters.

David had been in Africa for four years. He found himself increasingly drawn to the company of this gentle, deeply religious young woman. What David liked best about Mary was her acceptance of him and his missionary life. She was strong willed, had a bright mind, and skilled at being independent in the harsh conditions. As he thought about her, he realized he had fallen in love. He could not imagine a life without her.

In the pleasant shade of an almond tree David Livingstone asked Mary to be his wife.

David and Mary became engaged in May of 1844. After his rest and recovery from the lion attack, David returned to Mabotsa. The construction of a chapel was finished. His goal now was to build a home for Mary.

By September he had nearly finished the walls. He had laid out the foundation so the building would be slightly larger than her home in Kuruman—52 feet by 20 feet. He had built the walls of heavy stone a foot thick. The great mass would moderate the harsh temperature, keeping the building cool in summer and protecting against the chill of winter nights.

He wrote a letter to Mary: "The walls will be finished long before you receive this. Baba has been most useful to me in making the door and window frames. It is pretty hard work, and almost enough to drive love out of my *head*, but love is not situated there; it is in my *heart*."

To his family at home he described the work. "There is not a shop or store within five hundred miles. We must make everything we need from raw materials. We build brick molds from trees cut down and sawed into planks. Doors and window frames are made by hand. The natives' respect for a person depends upon the size of your house. You must have a house of decent dimensions. Most natives cannot help because they cannot set things straight. They make their dwellings round."

David returned to Kuruman during the Christmas season for the marriage. Robert Moffat, Mary's mother and sister watched, as did their many friends.

David wore his best clothes. He was nervous. He knew he could never find a better wife. He called her the best spoke in the wheel. Mary stood beside him, cool and confident in her crisp white dress and bonnet.

Rev. Prosper Lemue of the Paris Evangelical Society performed the ceremony. Robert Moffat entered the event in the Kuruman church record book with a flourish and great satisfaction.

Mrs. Moffat looked upon the marriage with misgivings. Like her husband she admired David Livingstone. But how would he balance the demands of being a husband with his strong desire to push deeper into Africa?

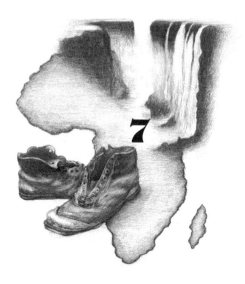

Mabotsa: The Marriage Feast

The people at Mabotsa held a special celebration to welcome back David and Mary. David said, "The village name, Mabotsa, means 'marriage feast'."

Mary was very pleased with her new home and the warm welcome from the Mabotsa villagers. But Rogers Edwards and his wife surprised her. They gave her a cool reception.

David said, "I know why the Edwards haven't welcomed us. Rogers Edwards has never accepted me as an equal. He treats me as a junior missionary. He believes our marriage will cause us to make Mabotsa our permanent station. He thinks of Mabotsa as his station."

Mary was astonished. "Everyone knows you are the leader," she said. "You can speak the language effortlessly. After all of these years Rogers still speaks through an interpreter."

"Rogers is right about Mabotsa," David said. "It is too small for two missionary families."

"What is the solution?" Mary asked.

David said, "You should not become too fond of your new house. We must leave Mabotsa to Edwards and find a new station of our own. I have always meant to go beyond the line of other missionaries."

Mary looked at the fine home David had built for her. Its construction had taken almost a year of his efforts. She had just settled in. "What of the house?" Mary asked. "You toiled so hard to build it."

"I'll give it to Rogers," David said. "The main chief in these parts is Sechele. He has his headquarters at Chonuane. I met him during my first tour of the countryside. Sechele impressed me by his intelligence and willingness to hear the Gospel. He knows me and will welcome us at his main village. I'll build a new chapel and home for us there."

"It will be frightfully expensive," Mary said. "When must we leave?"

"I'll tell Rogers and your father of my intentions right away. You can stay here until I build a home for you in Chonuane."

While they were still in Mabotsa, Mr. Moffat sent word that a hunter named Cotton Oswell would visit them. He had passed through Kuruman and the Moffats encouraged him to visit David and Mary. Even before he arrived, the natives were excited by the visit. It was a major event when a hunting expedition came their way.

David looked upon the visit with less enthusiasm. David never hunted for sport. Even killing game for food gave him no pleasure. Once, he waited in hiding for a herd of antelope to get within range of his rifle. He became fascinated with their beauty. He observed their habits as a scientist would. He forgot to fire when they drew closer. The natives came to see what could be the matter. They frightened the antelope away.

Cotton Oswell turned out to be a young man, thin but athletic, as if recovering from a long illness. His hunting party swept into the village, causing great excitement. He had three wagons, eighty oxen, several horses, and three hunting dogs. He had hired a large number of natives to take care of the animals and pitch camp when they stopped for the day.

He had to be incredibly wealthy, David decided. The expedition alone must have cost a thousand pounds, ten years of David's salary. He resolved to be civil to the man, but he could not imagine enjoying the man's stay at Mabotsa.

Cotton Oswell rode to the Livingstone's house. He immediately dismounted and took off his hat. "Doctor and Mrs. Livingstone," he said, "It is my great pleasure to meet you. I have some mail for you."

He shook David's hand and touched his cap as a salute to Mary. To her he said, "I've brought you some fresh fruits and vegetables—turnips, Jerusalem artichokes and apricots. Please accept them as a present."

To David he said, "I also have a bundle of recent newspapers from Cape Town. Would you care to read them?"

David eagerly accepted the package. Although they were several months old, everything they contained would be news to him.

Cotton Oswell's gentleness and sincerity charmed Mary. The young Englishman instantly won her over. Even David agreed that the man was not what he had expected. Although a wealthy man, Cotton kept careful records of his expenses. He was not wasteful. He didn't spend money recklessly. Yet, he freely shared what he had with David and Mary. Cotton Oswell reminded David of a description of what the best English schools sought to instill in the students. Cotton had been trained to always do what was brave, true and right.

David Livingstone and Cotton Oswell were from vastly different backgrounds.

David Livingstone grew up in a small, cramped apartment in a small town. Cotton Oswell lived in a fine, roomy house near London. During his early years David worked ten or more hours a day in the cotton mill. Cotton Oswell's childhood was free of labor. David attended the mill school after work. Cotton had a private tutor. David never had time for sports. Cotton excelled at all things athletic.

Members of Cotton's family held important positions in successful companies. One of his uncles was a director of the Bank of England. Like David, Cotton wanted to travel. His uncle found for him a job in India with the East India Company. While there Cotton learned the language. He became a key worker. He took his duties so seriously he overworked. He suffered a serious illness.

In England his classmates had called him "the muscleman." But in India, the fever left him in a sad condition. He weighed but one hundred pounds. Cotton Oswell took leave from his duties to recover. He decided to go on a safari to Africa.

He had to be carried aboard the ship to Cape Town. By the time he came ashore in Africa, he felt much better. His wandering took him to Kuruman where he met Mr. and Mrs. Moffat.

"They are the two best friends travelers ever came across," Cotton told David and Mary. "They insisted I should come see you here in Mabotsa."

Cotton asked for David's advice on back country travel and dealing with local people. David shared all he knew with the bright eyed explorer.

Cotton said, "I've heard reports through natives of a lake north of the Kalahari, called Lake Ngami."

David said, "Many have talked of finding the lake. Expeditions have been sent out, but all have grown discouraged and turned back."

Cotton Oswell questioned David about the lake's location.

Suddenly David asked, "Why do you ask about the lake? Do you want to be the one to discover it?" Finding the lake and proving that the Kalahari did not go on forever had been one of David's secret goals. Now that he was married it looked like he would never be able to fulfill his secret ambition.

"Not on this trip. I am not experienced in desert travel," Cotton said.

David said, "Desert travel is difficult but not impossible. The desert has many eatable roots and wild foods."

Cotton saw David's enthusiasm and knowledge of the subject. He said, "Should I come to Africa again, we will look for the lake together!"

"Yes," David agreed. "Your offer is an answer to my prayer."

After only two days Cotton had to leave. He promised to visit again. As the caravan rolled out of the village, David turned sadly away. Cotton was bright and fun to be around. David already missed his new friend.

Cotton Oswell could not have been more enthusiastic about the good Doctor Livingstone. Cotton wrote home, "In David Livingstone I have met the

best, most intelligent and most modest of the missionaries."

Near the end of 1845, David and Mary moved to
Chonuane. It was forty miles from Mabotsa. Their
duties fell into a busy pattern. It began with a family
worship and breakfast at the first light of the new day.
David then conducted an early school for anyone who
would attend: men, women, and older children.

When he returned, Mary asked, "How was the
class?"

David said, "The men and older boys had to leave
before we finished. It's the drought. The men have to
drive the livestock further and further from the village
to find good grazing land. It's a long walk and they have
to leave early."

Mary was gathering clothes to be washed. She
washed clothes by beating them with stones by the
river. They dried in the blazing sun. "If I get this
finished, I would like to make more candles. You have
been burning more of them lately. I need to make some
more soap, too."

David nodded. "I'll help." The soap was made
from the ashes of a local plant, the *salsola*, which he
gathered for her.

"I'll do it," Mary said. "There's a wagon wheel
that needs mending. And one of the natives left an ax
to be sharpened. He's working in the garden." The
villagers did little jobs in exchange for David's help.

"I wonder if he'll hoe in a straight line," David
said. He had to watch the natives' efforts. Otherwise,
they made everything round: walls, doors, windows,
fireplaces. Everything was round. They even dug cir-
cular graves.

Mary left with the wash.

"Will you be back for lunch?" David asked.

Mary said, "I don't think so."

David said, "We agreed you would take an hour rest at lunch." She was expecting a child. He did not want her to become too tired.

"I'll try," Mary said. "But the older girls want me to teach a class on sewing. It is quite popular and I do not want to disappoint them."

"But you have infant school, too," David said. "Sixty children. Can you do both?"

Mary said, "Can you do all that you do? You're the village smith, carpenter, gardener, preacher, teacher and doctor."

"But not dentist," David pointed out. Mary was better at extracting teeth than David. When someone needed a bad tooth taken out, they came to her rather than her husband.

After the long day, David and Mary got together to watch the spectacular sunset over the vast open land. It was a pleasant pause in the busy day.

After sundown, when the temperature became more pleasant, Mary went inside her new house. She had a few household chores to do—sewing, mending, and putting things away.

David walked into town. He watched the dreary line of men returning with their exhausted animals. It was a never ending march, from the watering hole to the distant grassland. After the men milked the cows and goats David held a public meeting. Sometimes he talked on religious subjects. At other times, he spoke on natural science and practical skills. He explained with diagrams and examples. When the natives learned of his interest in natural science, they brought interesting specimens to him. David would pack the specimens to ship to Professor Owen.

During the evening David would treat the sick. The last event of the day was a prayer meeting at Sechele's house. David tried to be home by 8:30 in the evening.

After Mary cleared the table, she asked. "Should I put out the light? Are you coming to bed?"

"Not just yet," David said. "I must make time to catch up on my reading." Although deep in Africa, David Livingstone kept in touch with events in the outside world. He subscribed to six magazines, religious periodicals, medical journals and the always entertaining *Punch*.

"Now that we have a home and a place to settle down," David said, "I would like to began building a library. Tomorrow a messenger will be going to Kuruman." David sat down to write an order for the latest books.

David told Mary, "Dr. Isaac Taylor has finished a new translation of Josephus. I'd like to order it. Also, I think we can afford a Greek New Testament and a Hebrew dictionary."

For his medical practice, David ordered a collection of essays by a successful physician, reference books on the diseases of Africa, and books on medicine and structure of the body. He asked the bookseller to find a cheaper, used copy of the writings of Hippocrates, a great doctor of ancient times. On scientific subjects he ordered books about the birds of Africa, a history of Egypt, and a book on lions and tigers.

His order would make its way to Cape Town and then to London. In a year or so the books would make their way to him, perhaps held in Kuruman for one of his visits. Or maybe a passing trader would haul them in his wagon to Chonuane.

As he finished the order, David told Mary, "My

first order of books arrived in pitiful condition. They should ship them inside a waterproof canvas pouch, tied with a strong rope. Instead, they wrap them in brown paper tied with a bit of string!"

One morning, Chief Sechele watched as David prepared for his morning class.

"What is this?" Chief Sechele asked. He was a person of great intelligence.

"It is the alphabet from which your words are sounded out."

"I will learn it," Chief Sechele decided. "Teach me."

Much to David's surprise, Chief Sechele did learn the alphabet. That evening David reported to Mary. "He really does want to learn to read. Every time I go into town he asks me to read the Bible to him. Isaiah is a great favorite of his. He has already learned the alphabet. He will be reading very shortly."

The chief always had a gift of food for David and Mary. Mary said, "Chief Sechele is a wonderful man."

The chief quickly learned to read and took to it with great passion. He read every book that Robert Moffat had translated into Sichuan. When he finished the books, he started reading them all over again. Moffat had sent a Sichuan language version of *Pilgrim's Progress*, which Sechele enjoyed time and again.

No one else in town showed as much interest in Scripture as their chief. He told David, "Do you imagine these people will ever believe by you merely talking to them? If you like I shall call my head man. He will whip them with rhinoceros whips until they all believe together."

David assured the great chief that people had to believe freely in God. The chief of his own free choice began to act according to what he learned from the Bible. He even tried to make peace with Chief Bubi, who was a rival. He sent David's old friend in Lepelole a gift of gunpowder.

A few days later a messenger came from Lepelole. Chief Bubi had been injured in a mysterious accident. David saddled a horse and hurried to his old friend's aid.

When David came back, Mary asked. "How is Bubi?"

"It is a sad story," David said. "For many years Bubi and Sechele were rivals who tried to control the Bakwena tribe. Finally, Sechele became the main chief. Chief Sechele sent Bubi a gift of gunpowder to put to rest their past differences. Bubi feared the gunpowder contained a charm. During his efforts to remove the charm, he brought some burning medicine herbs over the gunpowder. It ignited and the explosion killed him."

"How awful," Mary said.

"He was a good man," David said "and his people just as honest. During my months there I left my wagon unattended. Not a single item was taken."

David became more determined than ever to rid the people of their dangerous belief in spells. He convinced Chief Sechele that casting spells for rain making was wrong. Despite a growing drought, the chief told his people he would not chant for rain.

Sechele's uncle came to David Livingstone. He told David, "We like you as if you had been born amongst us. But we wish you would give up that everlasting preaching and praying. You see, we never get rain, while those tribes who never pray get plenty."

Others claimed that David had bound their chief with a spell. They pleaded for David to let Sechele return to his rain making duties. "The corn will die if you refuse. Only let him make rain this once, and we shall all, men, women and children, come to the school and sing and pray as long as you please."

David and Chief Sechele ignored the protests. Chief Sechele read the Bible now with a passion. He had not yet become a Christian. He did not know what to do with his wives. He had five wives. Three of them were the daughters of sub-chiefs. To send them away would not be easy. In addition to making their parents angry, the women had done no crime. A woman without a husband found it difficult to survive in the harsh African land. One of his wives, Makhari, had no family. How would she live?

"I have no fault in them," Chief Sechele said. "I am parting with them with the wish to follow the will of God." He gave them all the possessions in their homes and each new clothing. It was difficult for everyone.

For David, the most difficult moment was when he went to see Makhari. She was a sweet young woman and intelligent. She had learned to read. She always took part in David's classes. She would return to her tribe alone. Piled around her were the goods Sechele had given her. She melted into tears and fell into David's arms. In a choking voice, she offered back the Bible. "I must now go to where there is no word of God."

Chief Sechele was David Livingstone's first convert. It should have been a happy day. Instead, the triumph of the moment was darkened by the great anger the tribe directed at David and their chief. The people believed Sechele had betrayed their ancient traditions. They blamed him for the drought.

"The drought is terrible and getting worse,"

David told the great chief. "The whole continent is drying out. I believe the climate has changed. It has been going on for many years. We must all move to a better location with a dependable supply of water. The only way to water the gardens is to find a river. We will make a canal and irrigate the land."

Chief Sechele agreed. He decided upon Kolobeng as the new location for the tribe. It was by a river, about 40 miles away. The whole tribe moved.

For David and Mary it was difficult to move on. He had just finished Mary's house and the chapel. On his salary, it was difficult to build and abandon a new house every other year. He had worked hard to plant an orchard and build a protected garden. Now those would be left behind.

At first Mary and a few others stayed at Chonuane while the rest built dwellings at Kolobeng. But they soon had to leave. The village became unsafe. Lions stalked the streets at night. They roared in anger from the lack of food in the dried out countryside. She sent a message to David. He came with a wagon. They moved to Kolobeng. She lived in the unfinished house he had started.

Life in Kolobeng fell into the same routine as at Chonuane. David taught the men and older boys. He preached the Gospel and practiced medicine. Mary taught the girls how to sew and opened a children's school.

Mary and David now had two children. Robert was almost two years old. They had named him after Mary's father. Agnes was just three months old. They had named her after David's mother.

The house and chapel were built. Kolobeng took its place as the farthest missionary outpost. Sometimes David would think about his conversation with Chief

Sechele when they first met. "How will the people beyond the Kalahari learn of God?"

"Someone must bring the Gospel to them," David had said.

Chief Sechele no longer believed anyone could cross the desert. "Years ago rain fell more often. People experienced in desert travel set out when rainfall caused watermelons to grow. You would perish without them."

David kept a journal. He wrote in it those things he saw of interest. He used the little navigation training he had received to calculate the latitude of Kolobeng. It was 24 degrees, 38 minutes south. When he recorded the entry, he noticed the date. It was May 20, 1849. Eight years earlier he had arrived in Africa and set out for Kuruman.

As he closed the book, a messenger arrived with mail. David opened the canvas pouch. One of the letters was from Cotton Oswell. He was coming to Kolobeng. He wanted David to lead an expedition across the Kalahari in search of Lake Ngami.

8

The Land of
Rivers and Trees

Cotton Oswell arrived at Kolobeng ready to go exploring. He was fully recovered from his illness. He looked the part of a wealthy English adventurer—tall, good looking, intelligent, and full of action. Traveling with him was another Englishman, Mungo Murray, cut from the same cloth. Mungo said, "I've come along so Cotton won't have to write poetry."

Cotton Oswell's mind could never be idle. He could speak Sanskrit, Tamil, Persian, Arabic and French. He also knew Latin and Greek. Cotton wrote poetry to fill empty hours at night. At the end of the day if he were alone he would recall favorite passages he had memorized. Then he would translate them from one language to another and convert the passages to poetry.

At first Chief Sechele opposed their mission. He "You will be killed by sun and thirst." As the
~are with which Cotton had stocked the

wagons, he concluded that it might succeed. He appointed thirty of his people to go with David, Cotton and Mungo. Their mission was to bring back trade goods such as ivory.

David asked, "Will the additional people change your plans?"

"Not at all," Cotton said. "I have 20 horses, 80 oxen, a dozen Africans to control the animals, and supplies for a year." He promptly added Chief Sechele's men to his team.

Oswell took off his hat as Mary walked up. "Here is the good Doctor's wife. How are you doing Mrs. Livingstone?"

"Mary," she insisted. She was supervising packing a wagon with her belongings and the children's things. Mary was expecting a child, their third. She would go to Kuruman to have the baby while her husband explored across the Kalahari with Cotton.

The expedition moved out from Kolobeng for Lake Ngami on June 1, 1849. One of Chief Sechele's men had been to Lake Ngami. "It was years ago," David told Cotton. "How helpful he will be I cannot predict. The lake is real enough. The territory is controlled by a great chief to the north—Sebituane, chief of the Makololo."

The sun baked plain stretched off to the horizon. The wagon wheels sank into the sandy soil. The oxen struggled forward. The expedition only traveled early in the morning and late in the evening. In the severe heat of the day even the hearty oxen needed to rest. They covered only six miles a day.

One day during the noon break Cotton, Mungo and one of the natives went hunting. When it was time to start in the afternoon, they had not returned. The oxen plodded ahead. David made camp and still the men had not returned.

The next morning the three hunters showed up. Cotton explained what happened. "Everything looks the same, the same bright sunlight, the same cloudless sky, the same endless sand. You ride to a clump of bushes that looks familiar, but you can't be sure. You could walk within a quarter mile of camp and miss it. The perfect sameness of the country caused us to lose our way."

The oxen had been without water for two days. They were supposed to be at an oasis. The wells had filled in with blowing sand. There was no water.

David's practiced eye saw a faint shallow in the endless plain. He said, "This is the remains of an ancient riverbed. There is no water on the surface, but water may be just below the ground."

They all set to work with spades and turtle shells. Carefully they dug through the sand. Below was a hard layer that trapped water.

David warned, "Take care we don't break through the hard surface and let the water seep away."

Water began collecting in the hollows dug in the sand.

"This will be enough for the horses," Oswell said, "but not the oxen. What shall we do?"

David said, "We'll unyoke them so they can travel fast. We'll send them back to the last water hole. When they return here, the wells will have collected enough water for them."

"Good idea," Cotton agreed.

Natives drove the oxen back for 25 miles to the last source of water. When they returned, the wells were enlarged and full of water. The animals and humans had one last drink. They filled the water barrels and continued across the harsh desert.

Cotton chaffed at the lost time. "We lost ten days going back and forth between the water holes."

David said, "We should change our methods. You and I can stay with the main body of the expedition. Mungo Murray can ride ahead and prospect for water. He'll follow the ancient riverbed. A team of men will go with him, digging wells at regular intervals. We'll follow with the oxen at a slower pace. By the time we arrive, the wells will have filled with water."

The changes worked for a time. Then, one day they pulled up to Mungo's group. This time there was no water.

David asked, "Why did you halt?"

"The guide has lost his way," Mungo said. "There is supposed to be a depression near here where water collects on the surface. When the rain falls it actually becomes a marsh."

Suddenly, Cotton saw motion in the bush. "I think it is a lion," he said. Cotton jumped on his horse and took after it.

Instead, it was a Bushman woman. She tried to escape. Cotton galloped off in pursuit. David caught up with them. He tried to calm the terrified woman. He assured her of their good will. He still struggled with the Bushman's strange language with its tongue clicks. He gave her a piece of meat and some beads. She may not have understood his words, but she understood the gifts.

David explained their need for water. The little woman began walking in a direction away from their intended route.

"She's going in the wrong direction," the native guide said. "It's a trick."

David ignored the man. He questioned the woman more closely. He reported to Cotton, "She says we'll be there by sunset. That would be about eight miles."

"The oxen can't make it," Cotton said. "The distance is too far to pull the wagons. We'll unyoke them and let them go for a drink. We can come back for the wagons later."

The men and animals stumbled across the dry, flat desert. Suddenly, in the distance was a large body of water. Oswell grabbed his hat in his hand and waved it back and forth in triumph. He galloped off to the water. The dogs, horses, and natives all ran toward the waves dancing in the distance.

The Bushman woman looked at the excited men, puzzled. She shook her head, but they ignored her and raced off for the lake.

As David pressed closer to the lake, it seemed to get further away. Then the water dissolved. The vision changed to shimmering heat waves. They had been chasing a mirage. They came to a flat salt bed. Heat on top of the salt surface produced a perfect mirage.

Cotton asked David, "Were you fooled by it?"

"Completely," David promptly replied. "I thought we'd found Lake Ngami. We've gone three hundred miles. Surely it is not much further."

The Bushwoman had not been fooled. She had seen the image before. But she did know the way to a spring. The animals could smell the water. Soon the weary animals were full of water.

The next day was Sunday. One of the ways David observed Sunday was not to travel except in an emergency. The party decided to camp by the water and let everyone recover.

On Monday they came to a larger source of water. This was no mirage. It was a river, the Zouga. They followed the river to a native village. Some of the natives had heard of David Livingstone. He questioned them about the river. He told Cotton what he had learned. "The river flows into the salt pans where it evaporates and soaks into the ground. It disappears at that point. But its source is Lake Ngami. Instead of flowing into the lake, the river flows out of it. By following the Zouga we will reach our destination."

"How far is the lake?" Cotton asked.

David said, "It is still a long way off, maybe three hundred miles."

"We thought it was only three hundred miles from Kolobeng. Instead it is six hundred miles. We are only half way there," Cotton said.

David nodded. "Our water worries are behind us. We can follow the Zouga River to Lake Ngami."

Traveling by the river had a different set of hardships. They now had to hack their way through brush and trees forming a tangled growth along the river banks.

David and Cotton became more impatient to see the lake. After a hundred miles they came to a village on the river. The natives there confirmed that Lake Ngami was still a great distance away. This time, David and Cotton decided to slim down the expedition. They left behind everything except one wagon and set out at a fast march.

For twelve days they pressed ahead at a hard pace. On August 1, 1849 they came upon the lake. It disappeared to the horizon. David waded into the water. It was pure, clear and cold.

David observed, "Look, there's a native in a canoe. He's seven or eight miles out in the lake, and still he's pushing the canoe with a pole. That proves the lake is shallow."

The natives assured him that he and Cotton were the first Europeans to see the body of water. Oswell seldom wrote detailed reports of his discoveries. It fell to Livingstone to make a scientific record. To truly discover the lake, David knew he had to fix its position and describe it in scientific detail.

David set to work to make scientific observations. He took measurements from the only prominent landmarks in the area—two huge baobab trees. One was 76 feet around, a gigantic size even for baobab trees. He computed elevation by measuring the boiling point of water. The temperature at which water boils changes with the elevation. At sea level it boils at 212 degrees Fahrenheit. As elevation increases, the water boils at a lower temperature. Along the shore of Lake Ngami, David's calculations showed the lake to be about 2,100 feet above sea level. He checked the trocheameter, a device on the wagon that measured distance. Lake Ngami was 600 miles from Kolobeng. He used a sextant to measure the latitude, 20 degrees, 20 minutes south.

"What about longitude?" Cotton asked.

David shook his head, "My watch is not accurate enough. We are probably at 22 to 23 degrees east longitude."

As they explored north of the lake, they came to a wide river. "From where does this river come?" David asked the local people.

"From a country full of rivers—so many no one can tell their number—and full of large trees," they told him.

David immediately began making plans to explore the river. His eyes burned with excitement. "I think this is a tributary of the Zambezi. This river system could be the highway into the heart of Africa. I

must talk with Chief Sebituane of the Makololo. He can give us valuable information."

Oswell spoke of practical matters. "The hot season will soon be upon us. We must go back."

David still stood looking at the river. "Maybe we could build a raft. . . ."

"The river is infested with crocodiles," Oswell said. He took his friend by the arm and led him away. "We'll try again next year. I'll haul a boat up from Cape Town."

They turned back for Kolobeng. With the route well surveyed by David, and the wells still uncovered, they made rapid progress. Near the end of the trip, Mary sent a message to David to hurry to Kolobeng. She had given birth to a boy at Kuruman and named him Thomas. She and the three children had returned to Kolobeng.

David and Mary enjoyed a happy reunion. But he grew concerned because of the drought. He put a bulb thermometer three inches under the soil in the sun. After a few minutes he drew it out. The reading stood at 132 degrees. When insects ventured out of their holes at noon day they frantically looked for shade. Those that did not escape the sun's rays soon died.

The Kolobeng River was beginning to dry up. The natives had to drive their livestock for miles to find food and water. Sechele moved part of the people to Limaue, ten miles away, where native corn could be grown.

David fell back into his practice of doctoring and preaching. David was known throughout Africa for his skill as a doctor. He had a well supplied medicine chest. For instance he stocked it with chloroform, a recent medical discovery. In January 1849, Livingstone learned of the new chloroform. This anesthetic rendered people insensible to pain during operations.

David continued to bring the Gospel to the natives. They listened politely but then turned away. Chief Sechele remained the only Christian convert.

Chief Sechele said, "In former times, when a chief was fond of hunting, all his people got dogs and became hunters, too. If he was fond of dancing or music, all showed a liking to these amusements, too. But this is different. I love the Word of God, but not one of my brethren will join me."

David and Mary could now live in relative comfort. They had planted fruit trees—peaches, apricots, oranges, apples, olives and figs. In the garden they tried to grow ginger plants.

In the cool of the evening, David wrote letters home. He told Dr. Bennet about his disappointment that his seeds for medicinal plants failed to sprout. "I planted castor oil plants and also rhubarb and jalap. None of them grew." He asked his friend to send fresher seeds.

David wrote to Professor Owen to explain why he had not been sending any insects. The collection was in sad condition. "I placed the dried out insects in a tray, each one numbered with a tag about where it had been found. They became so dry in the air, the slightest shake caused them to fall apart. I've started over with a different method of preserving them. I now put them in jars filled with alcohol."

He also wrote to his sister Janet, telling her about the health of the family. "Four year old Robert is sitting by the window singing at the top of his voice. Three year old Agnes is crawling around trying to bite my leg. Thomas, the infant, is sleeping despite the noise." The two older children had learned to talk. They spoke both

English and Sichuan. To David, it seemed they were learning Sichuan better than English.

Outside, the natives banged on their drums and shouted and sang.

Mary asked, "How can you concentrate with the constant noise?"

David said, "My work at Blantyre's cotton mills prepared me well for this. I learned to read and think over the distraction of the mill and its constant clatter. I walked twenty miles a day between the spinning machines. Year-round they kept the building at 80 to 90 degrees Fahrenheit. Unknown to me, it prepared me for a life in Africa."

Communication had improved during David's years in Africa. Faster steam ships now crossed the ocean. His friend William Thomson from Anderson College in Glasgow worked as an electrical experimenter. He built improved telegraphs. The telegraph now flashed messages at the speed of lightning between the major cities of Europe. There was even talk of laying a transatlantic telegraph cable between England and the United States.

In less than six months of his return from Lake Ngami, the Royal Geographical Society in England received word of his feat. They recognized him as the chief scientist of the expedition. They awarded him the Society's Gold Medal. It was for "his successful journey, in company with Oswell and Murray, across the South African desert, for the discovery of an interesting country, a fine river, and an extensive inland lake."

The award also carried prize money, equal to about three months of his salary.

"What are you going to do with the money?" Mary asked.

David said, "For you, Mary, I shall order a special gift—a couch to be shipped from Cape Town to our home here."

Mary could not have been more pleased. But she did not want him to spend all of his money on her.

David explained, "There will be enough money left over for me to buy a watch of sufficient accuracy to fix longitude. I will use it on my trip with Cotton next year. I want to go back to meet Sebituane and his empire of the north and the land of rivers and trees."

"I'm going with you," Mary said. "My place is with you."

David saw her face in the light of the candles. She looked determined. He said, "Because you are expecting another child, Kuruman would be much more comfortable."

"You are my husband and my doctor," Mary replied.

David asked, "What of the children?"

"The children and the two girls who help me can go with us," Mary said.

David tried again, "What of the native school that you teach?"

"Until harvest is over, little missionary work can be done," Mary said. "Times are so harsh all hands must work. The natives labor every waking moment searching for food and drawing water."

David waited anxiously for Cotton Oswell's return. Would he bring a boat as he promised? By April of 1850 he had not heard from Cotton. "Apparently there is some mix-up," David told Mary. "Cotton should have been here by now. Further delay will throw our return trip into the hot season."

David faced a difficult decision. Should he go ahead now, wait for Cotton, or give up his goal of reaching the land of rivers and trees?

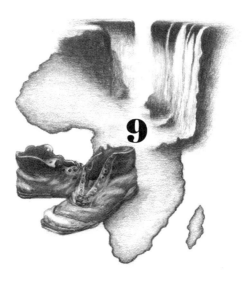

A Path to the Sea

"There has been a mix-up," David told Mary. "Cotton should have been here by now. We must not delay or we'll have to return in the hot season. We'll outfit our own expedition."

David's little band consisted of Mary, the three children, her two helpers along with David's old friend Mebalwe, twenty of Sechele's people and Chief Sechele himself. The goal this time was to meet Chief Sebituane about whom he had heard so much.

It should have been a relatively easy trip. David knew the way. The previous year they had dug wells that should still be full of water.

In Africa nothing turned out to be easy. Because of constant battles between tribes, a chief filled in the wells. Without water an enemy tribe could not make a surprise attack from the desert. To avoid being caught in the conflict, David swung away from the surveyed route. They once again had to eat desert food—

caterpillars, locusts, frogs and the roots of plants. Other than the strange diet, and a time or two when water came in short supply, the children stayed healthy.

About six miles from Lake Ngami, the party came to a village. Chief Lechulatebe welcomed David and his family. He gave them food and offered a place for Mary and the children to stay. David learned that tribes welcome an explorer who travels with his family. In Africa a man never took his women and children with him if he intended to start a fight.

David took his family to the lake. The children had been born and raised where water was a precious substance. The lake stretched away for miles, an astonishing sight to them. The children rushed to the water's edge. They dipped their toes in it. Within a few minutes they were playing in the mud and water like little ducks.

Mosquitoes rose in great clouds around the lake.

While David enjoyed showing the lake to his family, Chief Sechele bargained with Chief Lechulatebe on David's behalf. David needed canoes and guides to take him to Sebituane. The talks centered on David's gun, which Lechulatebe wanted. It was London made and very valuable. Chief Lechulatebe would settle for nothing but the rifle.

David returned from the lake. David asked, "What does he want?"

"The London rifle," Chief Sechele said.

David groaned. It was his favorite.

Chief Lechulatebe promised, "I'll give you everything you wish—guides, passage north, and boats to carry you. I will protect and feed your wife and children while you are gone."

Reluctantly David handed the rifle over. Despite the great cost, it looked like he would be moving north to his long sought goal. He told Mary the latest development.

She greeted him with terrible news. "The children have a fever. The two girls who help me have it, too." The children's bodies were covered with red sores.

Mary said, "Those are mosquito bites. The bites didn't seem that bad at the lake, but they got worse overnight. They may be the cause of the fever. What shall we do? Everyone is getting sick, even Chief Sechele's people."

David said, "I can treat them with quinine. But the best course of action is to leave immediately. The pure air of the desert will restore their health."

"You haven't seen Sebituane," Mary objected.

David said, "The children's health is more important."

David turned around and trekked south again. Cotton Oswell met them on the way home. As he had promised, Cotton had brought a boat from Cape Town. But the long ox wagon trip in the dry desert air had warped it so badly it was worthless. He broke it up for wood.

David arrived at Kolobeng in mid-August. Mary and the children were not well. The children could not climb down from the wagon without help.

A week later Mary gave birth to a girl named Elizabeth. The baby girl got sick, too. She cried fitfully. Little Elizabeth hung on to life for two weeks. Then she died. David buried her at Kolobeng.

Mary suffered a stroke. It paralyzed her right leg, arm and right side of her face. David took the entire family to Kuruman for three months. They spent Christmas and New Year's with the Moffats. The children ate good food including fresh fruit. Mary was able to rest and recover.

David avoided talking about his second trip to Lake Ngami. It had proven to be a disaster. His children were sick, his wife weary, and a newborn infant dead. He had not explored further north. He had not met Sebituane. He had gained very little new information. For David there was but one thing to do. Try again. He wrote to Cotton to set up a third try at reaching Chief Sebituane.

Mary learned that David and Cotton would travel north again the next year. She insisted upon going with him. "I shall go with you," Mary said.

"But Little Elizabeth—," David said.

Mary said, "Little Elizabeth's death was as likely to have happened whether I'd gone or stayed home. In the most civilized of surroundings your mother and father lost two children as infants."

David and his family returned to Kolobeng. The drought had gotten worse. Water no longer flowed in the river. Water collected in pits that the natives dug in the river bed. They watered the trees and garden. The trees survived, but not the garden.

Finally, rain clouds gathered, dark and heavy. The villagers danced in anticipation of rain. Suddenly, they scattered for cover. The clouds had finally opened. All that fell was hail. The huge hail stones slashed down. They broke the windows, damaged the roofs and destroyed the crops and grazing land.

Cotton arrived as David repaired the roof. David wondered if he should abandon Kolobeng. David said, "The drought is growing worse. The villagers must walk forty miles or more to take their herds to graze. The village is sometimes abandoned."

Cotton Oswell agreed, "Kolobeng has become

too dangerous for your family. Will Mary go to her parents at Kuruman while you are away?"

"She doesn't want to go there," David told Cotton.

Cotton hesitated. He believed David had unwisely allowed Mary and the children to go with him on his second trip. Cotton said, "Do you propose we bring her and the children with us?"

"Yes," David said.

Cotton sighed. He knew it impossible to change David's mind. Cotton said, "I'll go ahead by a few days march over the difficult part of the route. I'll clear the old wells and dig fresh ones."

The brave African explorers set out at the end of April 1851. They decided to by-pass Lake Ngami and head directly to Chief Sebituane and his Makololo people. A month later they came to the great flat salt pan. It was a hundred miles across.

They successfully crossed the salt pan. On the other side they found a Bushman who offered to be their guide. His name was Shobo. He claimed he could guide them across the plain to Sebituane's territory. He knew the Sichuan language only slightly.

While David struggled to converse with the man, Mary walked up. She burst into the Bushman language, speaking it rapidly and confidently.

David asked, "When did you learn their language?"

She said, "As a small child. My mother rescued a young Bushman woman who became my nurse. She helped raise me. I learned the language from her."

After several days of travel their new route took them to a vast plain of low thorny scrub. Shobo, the Bushman guide, looked thoroughly confused. He smiled, shrugged and spoke so quickly David had no

hope of following his meaning. "What did he say?"
David asked Mary.

Mary said, "He says he must confess that he is
entirely ignorant of our whereabouts."

Cotton said, "I didn't need a translation."

Shobo solved the problem by curling up and
taking a nap. The next morning he had vanished.

Cotton said, "So much for the Bushman and their
unerring knowledge of the African countryside."

By June 11 only a little water remained. David
saved it for the children. The entire company was in
distress. Then they came across a welcome sight—
dung from a rhinoceros. "Those are the droppings
from a rhinoceros," David told Cotton. "A rhinoceros
never strays far from water."

Quickly Cotton ordered that the oxen be unyoked.
The animals smelled the water and set out toward it in
a trot. Oswell and David stayed with Mary and the
children at the wagons. The rest of the troop followed
the animals. Overnight the children drank the last drops
of the water. The next morning David scanned the
horizon, looking for help. The wagons stood as a lonely
outpost on a vast dry plain. Not a bird or insect brought
life to the scene.

Mary sat in the shadow of the wagon. The children gathered around her, listless, hardly moving. With
parched lips they begged for water. David could hardly
bear to listen to the children's thin, painful cry. The
thought of his children perishing before his eyes was
terrible.

*Bringing them along was a mistake, a terrible
mistake*, David decided. He promised himself, *Should
they survive, I will never again put them through such
torture.*

In the afternoon some of the men returned with

enough water for everyone. David could hardly control his emotions. He was so relieved he nearly cried.

They learned they were near the Makololo town of Mababe. This town was under the control of Sebituane and on the Chobe River. "Our water worries are over," David said. "We shall reach Sebituane."

As they rolled into the village, Shobo the Bushman suddenly appeared at the head of the caravan. He marched into town as if he had successfully led them to their destination.

Soon the word came to David that Sebituane, chief of the Makololo, desired a meeting with them along the Chobe River. Cotton and David were taken by canoe about twenty miles up the river. Chief Sebituane had come four hundred miles to meet them. He greeted them on an island in the middle of the river.

Cotton put out his hand in the usual greeting of an English handshake. Chief Sebituane had never seen such a greeting before. He instantly recognized it as a sign of peace and friendship. He took Cotton's hand as if it had been his custom all along.

Chief Sebituane killed an ox for them and gave them honey as a welcome. Yet, the great chief had a strange look in his eyes. He acted ill at ease and frightened. He continued to lavish gifts on the two visitors. He gave them prepared skins of oxen, as soft as cloth. The chief said, "The greatest ambition of my life is to see a white man. This is the crowning moment of my career."

David explained the reason for the visit. "My goal is to preach the Gospel in this area and to bring the benefits of civilization to your people."

Late one night while David and Cotton slept by the camp fire, Chief Sebituane sat down very quietly by the fire. David and Cotton woke up. They greeted him.

The great chief seemed to be in a dream. Slowly, he recounted the events of his reign. It was as if he wanted to pass on to the two Europeans the details of his life before it was too late. As the fire flickered, he told about his wars, captures, escapes and conquests. Sometimes his voice was barely loud enough to be heard. At other times, it rose in excitement. Throughout the night he spoke. At dawn he stood and walked away before anyone else in the camp roused.

Cotton said, "That was the weirdest scene I have ever experienced."

David nodded. He had no explanation for the man's late night visit.

They traveled back to Mababe. Sebituane went with them. He wanted to meet Mary, the daughter of the great Robert Moffat, and Livingstone's children. Chief Sebituane was especially taken with Robert, David's oldest son.

On the first Sunday David held the usual religious service. The great chief attended. Sebituane was a man of great ability who ruled over an immense area. He readily agreed to give David whatever assistance he wanted to build a missionary station. Chief Sebituane said, "I will give you any part of this country to settle."

All of David's hopes appeared to be coming true.

That night Chief Sebituane complained of a chest cold. A few days later he was bed ridden and fading fast. David, being a stranger, feared to treat the great chief. Should his treatment fail and Chief Sebituane die, David could be killed along with his family and the rest of the expedition. David visited the man. He was relieved to see that Sebituane's medicine men were doing as well as could be hoped.

The next Sunday after services, David and his son Robert visited the sick chief.

"Come near," Sebituane said. "I am done."

One of his doctors said, "Why do you speak of death? Sebituane will never die."

David and Robert sat with the chief for some time. David told Sebituane about the mercy of God. Finally, David rose to leave.

The chief raised himself up a little. He called a servant. To the servant he said, "Take Robert to Ma-Unku, and tell her to give him some milk." Ma-Unku was one of his wives.

Chief Sebituane died during the night. David learned of the man's death the next morning. The act of kindness of giving milk to Robert was his last act and the last words he had spoken.

Despite the danger of being accused of somehow causing the tragedy, David attended the funeral. The chief's people dug the grave in the cattle pen. After the burial, the people drove the cattle over the grave until the animals completely trampled away its location.

The people asked David to speak. He said, "I urge you to keep together and support your chief's heir."

They nodded in agreement. "Sebituane has just gone the way of his father. Although the father has gone, he has left children. We hope you will be as friendly to his children as you were to him."

The successor was Ma-Mochisane, a teen-age daughter of Chief Sebituane. She lived several hundred miles away. After five weeks, she sent back word that David and Cotton could freely travel in the land of the Makololo.

David and his caravan struck north to Linyanti, a major town of the Makololo. They came to a great river on August 4, 1851. The size of the river stunned them.

It was more than a quarter mile across. It filled its banks even in the time of great drought.

"How glorious! How magnificent! How beautiful!" David said. "This is the Zambezi. I have no doubt."

The natives told them about an impressive sight down river. They called it "the smoke that thunders."

"Whatever could that be?" Cotton wondered.

David did not know. "Are they speaking of a waterfall?"

Cotton looked out over the Zambezi. "I cannot imagine this river making a waterfall. It would be an incredible sight."

"We must explore—," David began.

"It is time to head home," Cotton said quickly.

David looked over the broad expanse of the river. Reluctantly he agreed to start back.

The trip back was much easier. Rain brought a wonderful crop of wild melons in the desert. By September, David and his company reached the Zouga River. There he insisted they make camp. Cotton was used to David's decision not to travel on Sunday and thought nothing of it. But the next day David once again refused to travel, and the next.

"What is going on?" Cotton asked. "Why are we camped here? Come on, out with it! What's the matter?"

"Oh," David said. "Mary has had her baby." In the shade of a thorn tree, she had given birth to a boy. "Mary and the baby are doing well."

"Congratulations," Cotton said.

They named the baby boy William Oswell Livingstone after Cotton, whose full name was William Cotton Oswell. Little William quickly received the nickname Zouga, after the river.

They camped for eight days before moving on. During that time, David wrote letters home, transcribed his rough notes into his journals, and planned for his future.

David knew that the slave trade was on the rise in central Africa. Some of the Makololo wore faded cloth that could only have come from slave traders. Although no African would sell their own children, they would sell children they had taken during raids on enemy villages. The natives desired European goods such as cloth, tools and guns. Yet, they had plenty to trade other than slaves—ivory, wax, lumber, and an endless variety of products from plants and animals.

David told Cotton, "Once a real trade route is developed, the hateful slave trade will be brought to an end. Next year I'm going back to Linyanti. Then I'll explore a route down to the west coast."

Cotton said, "That's at least eighteen hundred miles. It's impossible."

David had already figured the distance. "I'm going down."

"Your family must return to civilization," Cotton said.

David agreed. "I'll send the family back to England. I have written the London Missionary Society describing my intentions."

David and his family stopped at Kolobeng. He filled a wagon with supplies and continued on the long journey. In March 1852 they arrived at South Africa's largest city: Cape Town. David had been away for eleven years. In his old clothes he looked like someone who had been stranded far from civilization, like Robinson Crusoe. Cotton came to the rescue once again. He generously bought David and his family new clothes and found them lodging.

The directors of the London Missionary Society agreed to his plan. They promised to provide for his family at home while he explored. They gave him a completely free hand in setting his course. The Society was not rich. He appreciated the trust they showed in his ability to spend their money wisely.

David placed his family on board a homeward-bound ship. Cotton paid for the tickets. David could not say enough good things about William Cotton Oswell. "He assisted me in every possible way," he wrote in letters to his family. "May God bless and preserve him! He was the best friend we had in Africa."

As they parted, David said he would join his family in England in two years. Almost as soon as they left, David wrote a letter. "My dearest Mary," he wrote. "How I miss you now, and the dear children! My heart yearns incessantly over you. I never show my feelings, but I can say truly, my dearest, that I loved you when I married you, and the longer I lived with you, I loved you the better."

They would be apart for two years, maybe longer. They left unspoken another possibility. He might march into the heart of unexplored Africa and never be heard of again.

The Raid on Kolobeng

David's goal was to scout a trail from the interior of Africa to the west coast. To succeed, he must accurately map his route.

David approached Thomas Maclear at Cape Town and asked for help. "I wish to learn how to make maps," David said. "I'm a missionary and doctor, not a mathematician and astronomer."

Thomas Maclear was the Astronomer Royal, the most eminent scientist in Southern Africa. He was a frank, friendly person. He said, "I must confess that I have grave doubts about being able to teach you on short notice. It is a specialized art."

David said, "I put myself in your hands."

David's quiet determination quickly won the praise of the Astronomer Royal. Thomas Maclear encouraged David and increased his confidence. "Your skill in taking observations with a chronometer watch and sextant is exceptional. You must reduce the observations to values for latitude and longitude. The calculations are long and tedious. Send me both your final results and your raw calculations. I'll double check your work."

David agreed.

While waiting for supplies to be delivered, David wrote about the geography of South Africa, articles on Christian missions and other manuscripts. However, not a single editor expressed an interest in the material. He put it aside. Maybe someday he would find a publisher.

David planned on opening trade routes with the people beyond Kuruman. He persuaded a Cape Town merchant to invest in the idea. The merchant chose a native trader, George Fleming, to go with David. George Fleming would start trading in ivory with the Makololo Africans at Linyanti.

David left Cape Town on June 8, 1852. He had a single wagon, enormously overloaded. All along the way to Cape Town, people had asked him to bring supplies back to them. These were his friends, so he could not refuse. His wagon creaked and groaned, protesting at being overloaded with other people's goods. One of the wagon wheels broke near Kuruman. David had to wait two weeks for repairs.

To his surprise Ma-Sebele, one of Chief Sechele's former wives came to Kuruman. Ma-Sebele had fled Kolobeng to escape an attack of the Boers, who were Dutch colonists that had settled in South Africa. She had her children and attendants with her.

Ma-Sebele told David, "When the fighting started, I hid with the children. We escaped to a little cave in the bluffs outside of the village. The Boers were firing right over my head. I could see the rifle barrels. An infant I was holding began crying. I was terrified the baby's cries would attract the attackers. I took off some of my beads. The child played with them and grew quiet."

"Are Chief Sechele and Mebalwe all right?" David asked.

Ma-Sebele nodded. "Mebalwe had church service on Sunday before the raid. Some of the Boers actually attended the service. The next day they attacked. Chief Sechele tells about it in his letter to Robert Moffat."

Robert Moffat let David read the message. "Friend of my heart's love," Chief Sechele wrote. "I am undone by the Boers who attacked me though I had no guilt with them. They killed sixty of my people, and captured women and children and men. They took all the cattle and goods. The house of Livingstone they plundered, taking away all his goods."

David read the letter again. He asked, "Why would the Boers do this?"

Robert Moffat said, "The Boers who marched away from Cape Town are unwilling to recognize the Africans as the real owners of the countryside. The Boers want to expand their land holdings and the number of native workers. They want to shut the country to everyone but themselves. Chief Sechele stands in their way. He allows missionaries and European hunters to cross his territory."

David said, "The Boers are resolved to shut up the interior. I am determined to open the country. We'll see who shall be successful."

David and his little expedition left Kuruman. A few days out they met Chief Sechele, a chief of one segment of the large Bakwain tribe. He sought justice. "I am going to Cape Town to see the Governor," Chief Sechele said. "If the Governor does not hear me, I shall go to London and put my case before the Queen. Will she meet with me?"

David could only admire the resolve of the chief to seek legal remedy rather than revenge. "Yes," David said. "I think Queen Victoria would see you. The problem is getting to London. The cost of travel and living in England is more than you can imagine."

Chief Sechele did make it to Cape Town. As David predicted, he could not raise enough money to go to England. He returned to his people.

David arrived at Kolobeng. He walked the streets. What he saw made him heartsick. The Boers had smashed his stock of medicines. He stopped here and there to pick up one of his books. They had torn out and scattered handfuls of pages. Loose sheets blew around in the wind. David found books he had bought from his meager salary at the cotton mill. Others he had ordered while in Africa and waited for months to get them from England. They were all now destroyed.

"If they had made use of my books and medicines I could have forgiven them," he wrote Mary. "But tearing, smashing and burning them is galling beyond measure." David could forgive almost any injustice against himself. The wanton destruction of his books would remain a disturbing memory all of his life.

David mourned for Chief Sechele's people. They had lost their corn, their cattle, their homes—and in some cases their lives. David took down the names of the children who had been stolen from the tribe. The Boers had taken the children to work in their homes as servants. The list had 124 names.

Many tribes had given in to the Boers' demands rather than risk war. This attack without cause frightened them. The Boers were becoming too powerful. The tribal leaders put aside their differences. They united against the Boers. Many of the smaller tribes joined forces with Sechele's people.

Rather than weakening Chief Sechele, the Boers had made him stronger.

Chief Sechele had ordered his people not to commit acts of revenge. The Boers did not know this. They became alarmed when the other tribes joined him. They sent four men to ask for peace.

All along the way, the four men saw armed natives standing in the hills over every pass. They agreed to the Bakwains' condition of peace, including the return of the children.

"This ended far better than we could have hoped," David told Mebalwe.

"But your books, your library," Mebalwe said, "it cannot be replaced."

David said, "I was wondering what to do with all of my possessions. Now the Boers have solved that problem. The plundering has left nothing here for me."

David and George Fleming started across the Kalahari Desert in December of 1852. This year he was pleased to find melons and sufficient water. He even saw large patches of grape-bearing vines. It turned out to be his easiest crossing ever. Along the way he had time to try out his surveying skills and to add information to his store of scientific knowledge. For instance, one morning he was awakened by the strange call of an animal.

"What is that noise?" David asked.

The natives said, "It's an ostrich."

David grabbed his stop watch and crept nearer to the bird. For years scientists had argued about how fast an ostrich could run. Suddenly the bird saw David and burst away, terrified. David started the watch and counted the bird's steps. The bird's feet moved so quickly they were almost a blur. He counted 30 steps in ten seconds.

He walked to where the animal had been and measured its stride. Incredibly, from one foot print to the next was 12 feet, an enormous distance. Now it was a simple matter to figure the speed. Multiplying 12 feet by 30 steps gave a distance of 360 feet. The bird covered that distance in 10 seconds. That would be 36 feet a second, or 25 miles an hour.

In the meantime the natives had snared one of the big birds. They cooked it for the evening meal. David ate ostrich that evening. It tasted like tough turkey. The eggs he knew to leave alone. They had a sulfur taste strong enough to turn one's stomach.

They continued on to the other side of the desert. The natives caught a tiny fly. They held it out for David to examine. Then they pointed to the ox and made a gnashing motion with their teeth.

David told George Fleming, "The natives claim this little fly can kill the oxen. It is a tsetse fly."

The effect of a bite was strange. Humans always survived a bite with no ill effect. Oxen would surely die, even from a single bite. David watched the progress of the disease in an ox bitten by a tsetse fly. The ox's eyes and nose began to water. The animal acted as if cold. Its jaws swelled. It lost weight and strength. Then, finally, it died.

The tsetse was not much larger than a common house-fly. It had the brown color of a honey bee. Tsetse were practically unknown south of the Kalahari. In central Africa the insect made journeys by ox wagon a difficult business. A native would walk with a switch by the oxen to help keep the deadly insect from landing.

They left the desert and now entered thick forest. Daily the jungle became more dense. They were kept constantly at work with the ax, cutting a path for the wagons. Finally, the forest opened. The country became very lovely. Grass grew higher than the wagon. Vines hung from the trees. David recognized wild dates and palmyra. Other trees were new to him.

Streams became more common. They crossed small rivers, sixty feet wide, but not very deep. The way became more difficult. The wagons fell behind because of the tall grass and many streams.

David told George, "I must find the Chobe River to follow to our destination. You stay with the wagons and I'll go ahead."

David and one of the natives set out on their own. They took a light pontoon boat with them. For a whole day they struggled through the grass and splashed in ankle deep water. That evening an immense wall of reeds blocked their path. The water was deep. David believed the river must be nearby. Far off in the distance he saw some trees on a rise of land. They made it to the trees at dusk.

While collecting wood for a fire, David came across a marvelous sight. It was a bird's nest made of leaves sewn together by the threads of a spider's web. He built a fire and they slept warm and dry.

The next morning, David climbed a tree. A sea of reeds stood between them and the river. He climbed down and they set out again. The reeds reached far over their heads. The heat and humidity made their progress stifling. Mixed in with the reeds was a type of grass with sharp saw-toothed edges. They struggled ahead. Only fifty yards separated them from clear water. Great masses of reeds eight or ten feet high blocked their way. They could not push into it.

Suddenly they came to a place where a large

animal had trampled down the grass. "Hippopota-mus," the native said.

The hippopotamus had pushed through to the river. The animal had made a way for them. At the river, David hesitated to use the little boat. He knew that hippopotamus happily tipped over canoes—it seemed to be a sport with them. In Africa, more people died from hippo attacks than from any other animal.

For the rest of the day they stayed out of the river and walked along its banks. They looked for a place to spend the night. Even a tree would do, but they could find none. Near dark they came to an ant hill with an abandoned hut built on it. They spent the evening in the old hut.

During the day David had seen water snakes putting up their heads as they swept around reeds in the water. Birds with long necks and slim bodies paddled low in the water. Only their heads and necks showed. Throughout the night they heard splashes, gurgles, and strange night sounds. Once, a loud noise kept David awake for an hour. "Another hippopotamus," he told his companion. He discharged his gun several times to frighten it away.

The next morning David decided they would have to put out into the river using the tiny flat bottomed boat. They paddled along, looking for signs of Sebituane's tribe. They also watched for hippopota-mus. They saw nothing but a few anthills rising above the wall of reeds on each bank. How would they safely spend the night?

As darkness fell, David saw lights from a camp-fire. It was a village of the Makololo.

The villagers ran to see the sight of the two men in the tiny boat. They welcomed them ashore and treated them as honored guests. The village elders could not believe David's exploit. "We thought no one could cross the Chobe without our knowledge, but you drop among us as if riding on the back of a hippopotamus."

David got his expedition back together. He located the rest of the men, wagons, and oxen. Makololo natives came down from Linyanti with canoes. They took the wagons apart and lashed together canoes to carry them.

Linyanti was a large village. Six thousand people lived there. The whole village welcomed the travelers. They all turned out to see the unusual sight of wagons, which they called houses on wheels.

Two years had passed since David and Cotton had listened to Sebituane tell the strange, rambling all night story of his life. Sebituane had died shortly after meeting David and Cotton. Before his death, he named Ma-Mochisane to succeed him. She was one of his daughters.

Ma-Mochisane had served as chief while David was away. She had not enjoyed her role. Her father had not wanted her to marry. Now she called a big meeting of the tribal elders. She intended to step down. She had two brothers, Sekeletu and Mpepe. One of them would become chief.

Mpepe came to meet David. He was anxious to be a friend. David learned why. Mpepe believed David had a weapon that would burn up any attacking party. The weapon was probably a cannon. Its destructive power grew as rumors of the weapon came from the south. Of course, David had no cannon.

The other brother, Sekeletu, was only eighteen years old. He was friendly and open to David. He took David aside. "Anything, either in or out of town, should be freely given if you would only mention it."

"All I wish," David said, "is the opportunity to teach you and your people about the Bible."

Sekeletu was not as skillful a leader as his father or even his sister. Even so, David preferred Sekeletu over Mpepe. David did not entirely trust Mpepe.

For three days the villagers met to select their new chief. In the end, it came down to which brother Ma-Mochisane preferred. She rose to speak. The people grew silent.

She said, "I have been a chief only because my father wished it. I always wanted to be married and have a family like other women. You, Sekeletu, must be chief, and build up your father's house."

An angry Mpepe returned to his village. There he secretly met with slave traders. They promised him guns if he would lead a rebellion. David and Sekeletu came to visit. Mpepe waited in ambush. He assumed the men would be afoot. However, David had given a riding ox to Sekeletu. When Mpepe saw the men on the oxen, he ran away, frightened at the sight.

That night, as the rivals met, David happened to sit down between the two. Mpepe had armed himself with a battle ax, ready to cut down his rival.

Just as Mpepe was about to strike, David stood. "The day's ride has left me tired," David said. "Where should I sleep?"

Sekeletu said, "Come, I will show you."

David stood between Sekeletu and Mpepe, spoiling the second attempt on Sekeletu's life.

During the night, some of Mpepe's men became frightened. Sekeletu had survived two attempts on his life. They believed he was charmed. They told Sekeletu of Mpepe's plan. Sekeletu's men grabbed Mpepe, led him away and executed him. David slept only a few yards away. It happened so quietly he never heard a thing.

The next morning David learned of the terrible deed. He frankly told Sekeletu that he disapproved of the bloodshed.

Sekeletu said, "By the chief, it is so." According to tribal law, the execution had been legal. Sekeletu had known of it and approved of it.

David often saw shocking sights in Africa. He never allowed his mind to dwell on the dark shades of people's character. The evil was there. But all around were scenes of beauty. He did not torment himself with those things he could not change.

They returned to Linyanti. David continued to practice medicine, make scientific observations and preach.

He held services twice each Sunday. Sometimes as many as a thousand people came. David would preach a simple sermon. He explained the plan of salvation, the goodness of God in sending his Son to die, the evil of sin, and God's commands. He kept it short and plain. The people listened with great care. A short prayer concluded the service. All kneeled.

David now prepared for his trip up the Zambezi and across western Africa to Loanda on the Atlantic coast. Twenty-seven of Sekeletu's men volunteered to go with him. They would take four ivory tusks. They wanted to see what ivory was worth at a port city.

Sekeletu gave Livingstone several riding oxen and as much food as the men and oxen could carry. David would leave his wagon behind. He would ride Sinbad the ox.

David reduced his gear to fit in five tin containers. The square metal cans were about fifteen inches on a side. He filled one with better clothes for his arrival at civilization in Loanda. He stocked the second metal box with his medicines.

The third box held his navigation aids. He had a sextant from London. A compass from the Cape Observatory. He also had a small pocket compass. His watch had a sweep second hand. He could stop the second hand without stopping the watch. This was especially important for making the exacting observations. He had a thermometer and a good small telescope. He could make the telescope steady by screwing its holder into a tree. Mr. Maclear had examined all the navigational instruments and pronounced them first rate.

The fourth box contained a "magic" lantern. It projected pictures to illustrate Bible stories. Into the final metal box he packed his books, a nautical almanac, logarithm tables and the Bible. This box also had his journal. The journal was a strongly bound volume of more than 800 large pages.

Other supplies included a few pounds of coffee, tea and sugar. He took a horse rug to sleep on, a sheepskin as cover, and a small tent. The natives had three muskets. David took a rifle and a double-barreled shotgun. He separated his gunpowder into several pouches to be spread throughout the whole luggage. He also carried twenty pounds of beads. He would trade the beads for additional supplies along the way.

As the little group marched out of Linyanti, David wondered if he had left anything essential behind. One item he must always keep with him—his wits.

A Man, An Ox or a Gun

David rode on Sinbad, an ox. Sinbad had a softer back than the other oxen and down turned horns. David rode in relative comfort without fear of being hit with the horns.

Although the ox never openly rebelled, he never accepted his role as David's riding ox. David guided the animal with a rope attached to a ring through his nose. When David pulled to the left or right, Sinbad would turn his head but keep going straight ahead. The animal seemed to know when David's attention wandered. If David looked away from the trail, Sinbad would go under a low limb to sweep David off. Sinbad would then kick his hind leg as if dislodging a pesky insect. Should his hoof strike David, so much the better.

The day's travel began a little before five in the morning. The natives cooked breakfast. They carefully washed the dishes, pots and hands before preparing food. David was anxious to get on the trail. The first two hours after breakfast were the most pleasant. They enjoyed fresh air and cool temperature.

He called a stop at eleven to eat and rest for an hour. The noon meal was meat left over from the previous night, biscuits with honey and a drink of water.

In the afternoon the heat became a problem. They stopped at the first good campsite. Game was plentiful outside Linyanti. Antelope grazed near humans because they had never been hunted with guns. At first, David let his men practice shooting. They missed so often he had to stop. They would have quickly run out of ammunition and powder.

Instead, David hunted and the men looked for fruit, wild honey, and eatable roots. From this they made the evening meal supplemented with their own coarse bread baked from maize meal.

David pitched his small tent a few feet from the camp fire. The oxen felt safer near the fire and would bed down around it. The men built little sheds made of poles and grass for themselves. In less than an hour, the camp became silent. The only sounds were from the jungle—tree frogs and the call of night birds.

David stayed up an hour or more writing in his journal. During the day he carried a small notebook. He jotted down his observations in it. At night he transferred the notes to his journal and enlarged upon them. He recorded latitude, longitude and elevation. He took weather observations such as temperature, sky conditions and rainfall. He noted new birds, animals, and insects—including a spider that bit him. He described the customs of African tribes.

If the nights were clear, David would take mea-

surements of the moon to fix their location. Sometimes he would pause for a final look around the camp. With a clear bright moon on the sleeping men and animals, it was a picture of perfect peace.

One of his last tasks of the day was winding his chronometer watch. Thomas Maclear had said, "Wind it to the same tension, at the same time and by the same person each day. This will ensure that it keeps better time."

Then David would crawl into his tent, kneel and say his prayers. He put himself and his men in the hands of God. He slept soundly.

They were in the territory of the Balonda. The main chief was Shinte. David came to a village whose chief was Shinte's sister. "Do not continue on your present course," she said. "Go see my brother."

From what David learned, Shinte's town would be out of his way. He rejected the change in his route. The woman chief had a daughter, Ma-Nenko, who was about 20 years old. The woman chief put her daughter in charge of changing David's mind. Ma-Nenko was a tall, athletic woman. She dressed by spreading animal fat over her body and then coating her body with a red powder. This and ornaments of metal, shells, bones and feathers were her only clothes. She carried herself as if elegantly dressed.

Ma-Nenko ignored David and instead talked to his men.

David ordered his men to load up and move out. "Pitsane, Kolimbota, Mohorisi," he called. "Tell the men to press on."

His men hesitated. "What's the matter," David asked Pitsane.

Pitsane, the Makololo head man, said, "She tells us that you will take us through a war-like tribe that will butcher us all."

"Nonsense," David said. Once again he ordered his men to move out.

Ma-Nenko flashed a signal to her people. They moved in and picked up the burdens. Ma-Nenko explained to David. "Your men can rest. Let my people carry your luggage to my uncle's. He will be angry if we do not help you."

David tried to leave. His men were already turning over the ivory tusks and luggage to Ma-Nenko's people.

Ma-Nenko put her hand on David's shoulder and gave him a motherly look. "Now my little man, just do as the rest have done."

David laughed. Here was a twenty year old girl treating him like he was a stubborn little boy. Visiting Shinte might be a wise idea. They'd left Sekeletu's territory. They needed to meet another strong chief who would sell them supplies and provide guides.

Ma-Nenko strolled along at a pace that kept the

others at a trot. David rode his ox, Sinbad, so he could keep up. It began raining, but Ma-Nenko pressed ahead.

"Why do you not stop and seek shelter from the rain?" David asked her.

She said, "It is not proper for a chief to appear weak." One of her porters had fallen behind. She went back and gave him a scolding that made him jump back in line. David and his men avoided offending her. A tongue lashing from her would cut deeper than any warrior's sword.

One of the Makololo gave Ma-Nenko his highest praise. "She is a soldier."

The rain continued. Water was in abundance here. Because of his years in the desert, David could not toss away water without a sudden impression that he was guilty of wasting it.

David suffered an attack of malaria. This disease has cycles of chills, fevers and sweating. In its worse stage he was racked with vomiting and painful diarrhea. None of his medicines made him any better. Finally, the attack ended, leaving him weak.

At the end of the third day, they came to Shinte's town. Ma-Nenko would not enter until she had sent messengers ahead. She explained to David, "It is polite to stop outside a village and send a messenger to explain the nature of our visit."

David took note of this custom. "Without you we would have blundered into town and perhaps caused an uproar," he told Ma-Nenko.

Shinte sent out a man to show them where they could spend the night. It was under a large tree near the center of the village. Two Portuguese traders had a camp nearby. They had a gang of young female slaves, a chain kept them together with iron bands around their ankles. They hoed the ground in front of the Portuguese encampment. It was the first time David's men had seen slaves in chains.

"They are not men," the Makololo said, "who treat their children so."

David had not seen slavery so openly allowed. He knew that the United States still had slavery despite an outcry from most of the rest of the world. Slavery and the trade in slaves had been outlawed in Great Britain for more than twenty years.

Chief Shinte had a little slave girl, only about ten years old. "It is my custom to present my visitors with a slave child. A great man should have a child to run errands for him. She can fetch your water."

David said, "I have four children. I should be very sorry if my little girl were given away. I would prefer this child to remain and carry water for her own mother. I hope you give up this practice of dealing in slaves."

"What can I do instead?" Chief Shinte asked.

"You can trade in cattle, ivory, and beeswax," David explained. "In those you are very rich."

Chief Shinte gave up trying to interest David in slaves. The chief did have one request, however. He had heard of the magic slides and wanted to see them.

David could not give the illustrated Bible program right away. He still suffered from malaria. There was a buzzing in his ears and he felt weak. He put it off for several days. This only increased everyone's interest in seeing the slides.

A huge crowd gathered for the presentation. The magic lantern projected pictures of Bible scenes. He could easily convey important truths of the Bible. One of the slides showed Abraham about to offer Isaac as a sacrifice. In the story, God ordered Abraham to sacrifice a ram instead. Everyone listened with silent awe.

David moved the slide out of the projector. The dagger in Abraham's uplifted hand seemed to strike toward them.

The women shouted in fear. They ran away.

Shinte, however, sat through it. David always showed how the projector worked, so no one would think it actually had magical powers.

Before David left, Shinte came into the tent. He closed the tent flap. In private he gave David the gift of a conical sea shell. For a tribe in the heart of Africa a thousand miles from the ocean, it was a treasure. He hung the shell around David's neck. "There, now you have a proof of my friendship."

Chief Shinte presented David an even more important sign of his friendship. He gave them food and guides for their continuing journey to the west.

"May God bless you," David told the chief.

At first David wondered if he would be able to speak the language of the faraway tribes. This turned out not to be a problem. As they left one tribe for the next, one language slowly merged into the next. The difference in dialect was close enough for him to learn the few words that changed.

They reached the point where Shinte's guides no longer knew the way and turned back. David and his men entered a time of unpleasant travel. They found no friendly welcome. They marched in pouring rain through miles of gloomy forest. The men expected to be attacked at any moment. David fell from Sinbad who gave him a swift kick on the thigh.

Every chief made demands of "a man, an ox or a gun." The expedition was down to only three oxen. They dared not give up a gun since it could be turned on them. David certainly would not give up one of his men. David said, "My men might as well give me as I give one of them for we are all free men."

Crossing the rivers in foreign territory was the most dangerous. Part of the company would be on the other side. Part would be in the middle of the river in canoes and part would be waiting on the near bank for their turn to cross. With the company divided like that, an attack was much more likely.

Shinte had warned David of the knife trick. A tribe would secretly drop a knife near David's camp. They would set a watch to see who picked it up. Then at the right moment they would charge the finder as a thief. The owner would demand the return of the knife and payment of a fine. This is what happened as they crossed a river.

One of the men of the village rushed forward crying, "One of your men stole my knife!"

David knew better. "My men are honest."

The unlucky young man who had found the knife came forward. "I have the knife."

The young man returned the knife, but the owner demanded a fine. The young man who had found the knife offered some beads. The owner demanded more. Finally, the young man gave up a fine shell which he carried around his neck.

They entered the territory of the Chiboque. This tribe was especially warlike. Men and women both sharpened their teeth to points. It gave them a fierce appearance. The chief was Njambi. They camped outside his village on Saturday. David wanted to avoid the tension of another confrontation with an angry chief. He slaughtered an ox and sent some of the meat to Njambi. David hoped to enjoy a quiet Sunday.

The next day the chief sent a little meal—far less

than custom would require—and demanded "a man, an ox or a gun." Njambi's warriors surrounded the camp. They came armed with swords. Some of the Chiboque whispered, "They have only five guns."

David's men seized their spears and stood ready to defend themselves. David sat on his camp stool. He held his double-barreled gun across his knees. He invited the chief and his head men to be seated on the grass.

Once seated, Njambi stated his demand for tribute: a man, an ox or a gun. "Without it I will prevent you from making any further progress," the chief said.

David said, "We are ready to die rather than give up one of our number to be a slave."

"Then you can give a gun," the chief said.

David said, "You are intent on plundering us. Giving a gun would help you to do so."

"No," the chief said. "All we want is the customary tribute."

David told the chief, "If we trod on your gardens we would pay, but not for marching on land which is still God's and not yours."

David's men earnestly asked him to give something. By now the expedition had hardly anything left. David parted with one of his shirts. He found some beads to put with it. The chief's head men angrily refused. David added a large handkerchief. Their demands became more unreasonable. They gave their swords a threatening shake.

David heard a noise behind him. He turned to find one of the natives charging him. David brought the muzzle of his gun around and put it in the man's face. The man retreated. David wanted to avoid any fighting. His men were confident and brave. They would win any fight even when out-numbered and out-armed. But he did not want to shed blood. He wanted to return the Makololo safely home.

David told Chief Njambi, "Everything has failed to satisfy you. It is evident that you want to fight. We only want to pass peaceably through your country. You must attack first and bear the guilt before God. We will not fight until you strike the first blow."

Suddenly Chief Njambi realized he had been tricked into sitting down before David. Chief Njambi and his head men would be defenseless sitting on the grass. The chief said, "You come among us in a new way and say you are quite friendly. How can we know it unless you give us some food, and you take some of ours?"

David gave them the rest of the ox. He received in return that evening a very small basket of meal—again far less than custom would require—and two or three pounds of the same ox. But the crisis was past.

Their route took them to a beautiful valley. It was about a hundred miles across, clothed with dark forest, and here and there meadow lands. On the opposite side rose a range of lofty mountains. A cloud passed across the middle of the valley, from which rolling thunder pealed. At the same time sunlight shone upon them.

"It is a glorious sight," David said.

But the rains continued. Metal tools needed to be regularly oiled or they became rusty. Clothing mildewed and fell apart. Shoes became moldy and the soles separated. David's tent gained a new rip every time he set it up.

David's men became discouraged. David was in his tent suffering through another attack of malaria. The men talked together. They called David out. Mohorisi said, "We have decided to turn back."

David looked at Kolimbota, Pitsane and the others.

They nodded in agreement with Mohorisi. David said, "We are near Portuguese settlements where our problems will be over. If you return I will go on alone."

He returned to his little tent. He prayed. He recorded part of the prayer in his journal. "O almighty God, help, help! Leave not these wretched people to the slave-dealer and Satan!"

David went to sleep not knowing what the morning would bring. Would he awaken to an empty camp?

The next morning someone pulled back the flap of his tent. It was Mohorisi. He stuck his head in and said, "We were discouraged in dealing with people who demanded slaves. We will never leave you. Do not be disheartened. Wherever you lead, we will follow."

One by one the men came to the tent and repeated Mohorisi's pledge. "We will never leave you. Wherever you lead, we will follow."

That night David could write, "They are all right again. I thank God for it."

They had one final river to cross to enter Portuguese territory. It was rumored to have venomous water-snakes and hippopotamus. David tried to interest the local people in carrying them to the other side in canoes. Their chief made an appearance. His warriors carried guns. "All the river men are my subjects," the man said. "They can do nothing without my say-so." He demanded payment. It was the same story—"a man, an ox, or a gun."

David and his men simply had nothing else to trade. David was tired of the constant bickering. He decided to march away and seek canoes elsewhere.

The tribe fired upon them. Luckily, they could shoot no better than David's men. The bullets fell short of the target.

Help arrived in the form of a young Portuguese

sergeant, Cypriano de Abrao. He found a way across the river and welcomed them to Angola under full Portuguese protection. Now it was merely a matter of surviving the next four hundred miles to Loanda.

After resting and eating real food at Cypriano's house they set out again. In a few days they came to Cassange, the first real town. It was the most remote station of the Portuguese in Western Africa. David was wet, his clothes in tatters, so undernourished that he looked near starvation. Malaria had racked his body so he could hardly walk. When he limped into the town, an old gentleman stopped him and demanded his passport!

"Without a passport you must appear before the authorities," the man said.

David felt so ill he would have gladly welcomed a prison bed and prison food. He followed the man to the commandant. David showed the commandant his passport and stood uneasily waiting for his fate.

The commandant said, "Dr. David Livingstone. I am about to eat supper with several friends. Will you honor us with your presence?"

David agreed because he was ravenously hungry. David told those at the table, "The fever on occasion caused me to forget the day of the week, the names of those who traveled with me. I think, had I been asked, I could not have told my own name."

One of the men kindly invited David to spend the night in his house. The next morning, David found clean clothes laid out for him. David now went out to take care of his men, but found they had also been furnished with food.

Cassange was a small village, only about forty buildings. The villagers watched David making notes and taking the latitude and longitude. They concluded that David must be a secret agent.

They said, "You must be more than a missionary to know how to calculate longitude! Come, tell us at once what rank you hold in the English army."

Despite their suspicions about his real reason for being in Cassange, they were kind and hospitable.

The time now seemed right to sell one of the ivory tusks. The Makololo men got a very satisfactory price for it—two muskets, three small barrels of gunpowder and enough calico to make new clothes for the whole party. They sold another tusk for additional calico cloth. It was a medium of exchange and would be used to pay their way down to the coast.

David continued to battle malaria. He became so dizzy he sometimes nearly fell from the ox. He was so weak that he could not walk unaided. His companions supported him. "It is annoying to feel so helpless," David said. He was near death.

They came over a rise and beheld the sea. The Makololo were dumbfounded. Coming from the desert, they had always imagined the world as land that went on forever. They said, "We believed that the world has no end. But all at once the world said to us, 'I am finished; there is no more of me!' "

The closer David got to Loanda, the weaker he became.

He had been told at Cassange that Loanda had no hotels and no hospitals. The city had but one Englishman. The English gentleman was Edmund Gabriel, British Commissioner for the suppression of the slave trade. Somehow David made it to the man's house. He was delighted to see that this was a true Englishman—he grew flowers in boxes on his porch.

Once safely in the hands of Edmund Gabriel, David could collapse. He fell into bed and was soon asleep.

The Smoke that Sounds

The next morning David enjoyed the luxury of sleeping late. He awoke in a real bed and not on the ground. Malaria continued to rack his body. Loanda had no hospital. It did have British naval vessels at anchor in the harbor. Mr. Gabriel appealed for their help. One of the naval surgeons prescribed quinine. David began a slow recovery.

Edmund Gabriel offered to write letters for him. David dictated a letter to the directors of the London Missionary Society. He asked them to tell his family and friends of his safe arrival.

David asked, "Mr. Gabriel, are there any letters from my wife?"

Edmund Gabriel said, "Sadly, no. You do have messages from others in England."

From those letters, David learned that Mary and the children had made it safely to England. Mary strove to keep the family together on the small sum the London Missionary Society could afford to give her.

David asked, "How are my men, the Makololo, doing?"

Edmund Gabriel said, "They are having a fine time. When they saw a large building with many rooms they said, 'It is not a hut. It is a mountain with several caves in it.' They make no secret of their awe of the sights around town or of the ocean. When you are well enough, they would like to visit a ship."

David took the Makololo aboard the ship *Pluto*, under the command of Norman Bedingfeld. Cautiously the men climbed the rope ladders up its side. They still feared being taken as slaves. The sailors welcomed the men. They said, "We have been sent by the Queen of England to prevent the buying and selling of black men."

The sailors gave the Makololo a meal of bread and meat. The Makololo's fears vanished. The sailors took them all over the ship. They explored the decks, climbed the rigging, and went down in the hold of the ship. The highlight for them came when they got to fire a cannon. As they left, the Makololo said, "It is not a canoe at all. It is a town!"

The Makololo learned that the people in town would pay for firewood. So they hiked out into the country, collected firewood and returned to the city. Soon they had set up a brisk trade in firewood. They made a good wage.

A ship arrived loaded with coal for other British vessels that were steam powered. Mr. Gabriel hired David's men to unload the coal. They were amazed at the "stones that burn." The size of the ship staggered them. It held so much coal it took them a month to unload it.

In the meantime, David had been putting together letters and reports of his journey. Some of his reports went to the London Missionary Society, others to the Royal Geographical Society, still others to the College of Surgeons. He wrote letters to all of his friends—Cotton Oswell, Professor Owen, Professor Young and many others.

He wrote a letter to Mary and the children. "I long for the time when I shall see you again. I hope in God's mercy for that pleasure. How are my dear ones? I have not seen any equal to them since I put them on board ship. My brave little dears! I only hope God will show us mercy."

Mr. Gabriel asked, "Dr. Livingstone, would you like me to arrange passage for you back to England?"

David shook his head. "The temptation to rejoin my wife and children is great. Nevertheless, I must refuse. My goal was to find a path to the sea for European trade. The way from Linyanti is extremely difficult, with rivers and marshes that are not suitable for wagons. I must go back and seek a path the other way, east to the Indian Ocean."

Mr. Gabriel looked as if David had taken leave of his senses. "Since June 1853, you've traveled from Cape Town to Linyanti and then here to Loanda. That's a distance of about 2500 miles. You'll have to retrace your route back to Linyanti and then go to—"

"To Quilimane, I expect," David said.

"That's another 1500 miles!" Mr. Gabriel said.

David said, "It will be impossible for my men to return alone. The tribes between Cassange and Shinte's territory are too unfriendly. I promised Chief Sekeletu that I would bring them home safely. Then I will blaze a route to the Indian Ocean."

Mr. Gabriel said, "At least wait for the mail ship

Forerunner. It is scheduled to arrive soon—in about a month. Wait and put your dispatches safely aboard the ship." Mr. Gabriel hoped the delay would cause David to change his mind.

David did agree to wait for the mail ship. His reason was not merely to see off his precious dispatches. Maybe the mail packet ship would have letters from Mary. After a month the ship arrived but with no mail from Mary.

The city's people bought the Makololo new robes of blue and red striped cotton cloth and red caps. They packed a military uniform for Chief Sekeletu. The sailors made David a new tent of strong canvas. His men called it David's 'house of cloth.'

David drew seventy pounds against his missionary salary. He bought cotton cloth and beads for trade. He took a collection of fruit trees and vegetable seeds. He bought two donkeys because he had heard reports the tsetse did not infect them. He also bought a musket, lead bullets and gun powder for each of his men. For himself he had a large hunting rifle and a double barrel shotgun.

They set out on November 3, 1854. The Makololo had become wealthy during their stay in Linyanti. They could not carry all the goods they had bought. For the first part of the trip they hired 20 porters to help them carry everything.

The trip back began as a pleasant excursion. Edmund Gabriel accompanied them. Bright sunlight shone on a cheerful countryside looking fresh and green.

Near Cassange, they met Colonel Pires, a wealthy landowner and merchant. Colonel Pires welcomed them with a great outdoor feast. He slaughtered an ox for the occasion.

That night, David suddenly awoke. He was being bitten by Africa's red army ants. The bites were like sparks of fire. David jumped about for a second or two, then in desperation he tore off his clothes.

"Ugh!" David said. He looked around. Fortunately, no one saw his crazy dance. If they had, they probably would have thought him mad. It astonished him how such small insects could cause such pain. They not only bit him, but they twisted themselves around after setting their pinchers in his flesh.

David noticed some natives around the uneaten portion of the ox. They kept a ring of straw burning around the ox meat. David investigated. The natives explained the army of ants could cut up and carry away most of an ox in one night. The natives would stay up all night to keep the ring of fire burning. Otherwise, the ants would devour all that remained.

The next day David saw the army ants on the move. From a distance, they appeared as a red colored band, two or three inches wide. Up closer he saw the band to be a seething mass of ants. Should a lizard or mouse be in their path, they would attack and devour it, reducing it to a skeleton in minutes.

David marveled at the wisdom of God's creation. He could see God's purpose in making the red ants. "They are very useful in ridding the country of dead animal matter," he wrote in his notes. "When they visit a human habitation, they clear it entirely of vermin. They destroy many harmful insects and reptiles. They are unafraid to attack rats, mice, lizards and even the python snake."

They entered Cassange. It was the last Portuguese outpost. A package caught up with him. It had still another gift, a six-barreled revolver.

The package also had newspapers. The *Times* of London told of the outbreak of the Crimean War. David believed Cotton Oswell and another of his friends, Thomas Steele, might be involved. The newspaper told about the charge of the Light Brigade. The papers carried only the first part of the story. The seven hundred English cavalry charged the Russian lines in the face of cannon fire in spite of being vastly outnumbered. To learn how it turned out he would have to wait until he arrived at civilization on the other side of Africa.

Even David made the *Times*. A news item described Livingstone's journey to Loanda as "one of the great geographic explorations of all time."

David looked up to find Colonel Pires waiting with difficult news. The Colonel said, "The packet ship *Forerunner* has gone down at sea. Everything aboard was lost."

David sagged at the news. "My maps, journal, dispatches, letters—"

"All lost," Colonel Pires said.

"I'll have to rewrite them," David decided. He stayed in Cassange and began the task of reproducing all he had done in Loanda. Fortunately, David had kept the notebooks filled with rough jottings. He had used these to write the journal. The notebooks, along with his exceptional memory, helped him recover his lost papers.

With that task behind him, he said farewell to civilization and set out for Linyanti. It was New Year's Day, 1855.

They passed through the region of unfriendly natives with only one incident. David heard his men at the back of the line cry out. They were being attacked.

Warriors knocked the burdens off their heads and tried to steal them.

David raced back along the path with Pitsane. David carried his six-barreled revolver. The chief looked wide-eyed at a gun. He cried out, "Oh! I have come to speak to you, and wish peace only."

David said, "Go away home to your village."

The villagers seemed pleased to do so when they saw that each of David's men carried a musket.

Beyond that point, the people were more friendly. The expedition stayed nearly every night in a native village. Many of the villagers had heard of the Europeans with their white skin, but never seen any. Some native mothers used white people as hobgoblins. She would tell her children that if they were bad, a white man would come and bite them. When David entered a village, the children who had been bad would run screaming from his sight.

David continued to ride Sinbad, although the animal barely tolerated him. David would try to hold up an umbrella to keep off the sun or rain. The animal would stumble causing David to tumble to the ground. The same thing happened when he tried to hold a book. David needed both hands to ride Sinbad.

David discovered another small lake, the Dilolo. From one end it overflowed into the Kasai River. The Kasai flowed west and eventually emptied into the Atlantic Ocean. At the other end of the lake, the water overflowed into the Zambezi and made its way to the Indian Ocean. Most great rivers have their headwaters in lofty mountains. Yet the Zambezi began on level ground. Here on this flat plain, far from any towering mountains, was the watershed of Africa. It divided the continent. Locating the watershed is an important geological discovery.

They were seeing familiar faces once again. At Shinte's village David planted some of his fruit trees: orange, cashew, fig, coffee and papaw.

Shortly before they reached Ma-Nenko's territory, they came into a tsetse fly region. A man walked behind Sinbad with a branch and kept the tsetse from alighting. Despite this measure, one of the insects bit the ox. The next morning sore and inflamed spots marked the tsetse bites.

Sinbad would die.

David assumed that the animal would be killed and eaten for food. But his men had grown attached to the cantankerous ox. They led Sinbad away so David would not be present when the poor animal expired.

On September 11, 1855 David and the Makololo arrived at Linyanti. It had taken a little less than a year to make the journey from Loanda. With a great deal of satisfaction, David returned all the men home. He had lost not a single one of the twenty-seven men. He returned all of them in good health.

The next morning was Sunday. The village of six thousand observed a special day of thanksgiving. David's Makololo men had saved their fine clothes from Loanda. They looked quite impressive in their new robes and red caps. The men came to the service and sat brave and straight like the soldiers they had seen in Loanda.

Chief Sekeletu wore the fancy military uniform sent to him by the people of Loanda.

At the church service, David told about the goodness of God in preserving them from all the dangers of strange tribes and diseases. He said, "The Word of the Living God has life and power. Few human hearts can withstand its force, and no hatred, however deep, can quench its power. I bless God from the bottom of my heart for allowing me to sow the good seed."

Pitsane then rose and described their exciting adventure. He told everyone about the kindness of Mr. Edmund Gabriel and the English sailors.

On the way back David had traded away most of his goods. He returned to Linyanti as poor as when he left.

Robert Moffat had made up a box for David and sent it from Kuruman to Linyanti. Mrs. Moffat forwarded white shirts, blue coat, woolen socks, lemon juice, jam, tea and coffee. Some of it had come all the way from Hamilton in Scotland. In the box was a copy of a letter from Thomas Maclear, the Astronomer Royal at Cape Town. "I do not hesitate to assert that no explorer on record has determined his path with the precision you have accomplished."

David now put together his expedition to go east. More than a hundred of the Makololo volunteered to go with him. He explained that this time he would not be able to bring them back. He would catch a ship at Quilimane and at last see his family.

After six weeks in Linyanti, they set out on October 27, 1855. Pitsane and Mohorisi decided to go with him. Two other experienced men joined the expedition—Sekwebu and Kanyata. Sekwebu had traveled part of the route and understood the dialects spoken along the way.

For a time Chief Sekeletu accompanied him, bringing the total number of people in the expedition to 200. Their first goal was the "smoke that sounds." David had heard of this great waterfall. The entire Zambezi River fell into a giant crack in the earth, disappearing from sight. Only the huge columns of mist could be seen. From a distance it looked like smoke.

They came to a patch infested with tsetse. The tsetse did not fly at night. David said, "Let's take the oxen and other animals across after dark."

Most of the men would go ahead by daylight and make camp.

David and Chief Sekeletu, along with 40 young men, would wait outside the tsetse area until nightfall. They began the cattle drive at ten o'clock. It was pitch dark. A storm came up. Sheets of lightning covered the sky. The whole countryside would be briefly lighted and then plunged into complete darkness.

The horses trembled and turned about. Every new flash revealed the party going in different directions. The men stumbled over each other. The young men began laughing. The thunder was deafening. Their laughter changed to cries when a very cold rain began pelting them.

They gave up trying to make it to the camp and stopped for the night. David had sent his pack ahead so he had no tent and no dry clothes. Chief Sekeletu covered him with his own animal skin blanket and lay uncovered himself.

Chief Sekeletu continued with David until they reached the "smoke that sounds." One morning as the expedition set out, David saw columns of smoke rising. Sometimes the natives burned the grass to help new crops grow. This looked like a range fire. But as he drew closer, he saw the columns of water vapor. It was a waterfall.

About a half mile from the falls, David got in a light canoe. The men would paddle him to an island at the edge of the falls. They had done this before. Even so, it was a difficult and dangerous ride. They could be swept away by the fast flowing current. They shot out into the center of the broad river. Rocks rising above the surface of the water caused eddies and still spaces. By moving from one to the next they made it to the island.

Carefully, David crept with awe to the edge of the island. It looked as if the land had been torn apart. The great river fell into the deep but narrow canyon. The thundering water sent up a dense white spray. Two bright rainbows gave it a magical look.

David tried to estimate the size of the spectacle. How wide was the river? How deep the falls? He knew he was a poor judge of distances over water. While in Loanda, he estimated the distance to shore while aboard a ship. He estimated it to be twelve hundred feet and it turned out to be more than twice as far. In vain he tried to remember how to measure the width of a river with the sextant. He could remember that it was easy, but he had forgotten how to do it. It was very vexing.

He estimated the river to be 3000 feet wide and the falls a 100 feet deep. He knew the river could be as much as 6000 feet across—more than a mile. The falls could be 200 feet—maybe more. Regardless of its size, this was one of the great wonders of the world.

David did not give English names to the country-side like other explorers. But in this case, he made an exception. He gave the name Victoria Falls to the astonishing sight. Queen Victoria was the monarch of Britain.

The next day he braved the dangerous current again to return to the island. Chief Sekeletu came with him. A great variety of trees covered the island. David said, "I believe the seeds have been washed down stream from the distant north. Several of these trees I've never seen before." It was as if the river's tributaries

were exploring for him—bringing down seeds where he had never set foot. He took notes of the trees. The whole scene was extremely beautiful. Some of the trees had blossoms. The great burly baobab trees grew around the edges. Graceful palms rose into the blue sky and spread their feather-shaped leaves.

The excitement of the scene filled David with a sense of wonder. Truly, he was far from home.

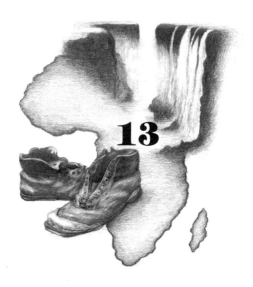

A Hundred
Thousand
Welcomes!

Going east, David entered a region that had been
ravaged by war. It was here that his wife Mary as a
young girl had escaped from one of Shaka Zulu's war
parties. Even after Shaka's death, chiefs and warriors
from one village fought against those in other villages.
They only stopped fighting each other to mount a
combined attack against the Portuguese. Ordinary
people wearied of the constant conflict.

One woman told David, "We are tired of fight. It
would be pleasant to sleep without dreaming of anyone
chasing me with a spear."

David rejoiced that the people seemed ready to
learn of Jesus, the Prince of Peace. He described how
at Jesus' birth the angels told the shepherds, "Peace on
earth and good will to men."

The women here pierced their upper lip and put a shell in the opening. They continued to put in larger and larger shells until the lip was as big as a person's hand.

Sekwebu said, "These women want to make their mouths to look like those of ducks."

Each village welcomed David and his men. The young women were especially pleased with the new dance steps the young men showed them. They said, "Dance for us and we will grind corn for you."

David noticed that his young men came up with dances that he had never seen.

In going to Loanda they had marched through the rain. Now David believed getting wet brought on malaria attacks. When he saw a storm coming, he halted. The men made grass shelters for themselves and started a big fire. David would sit on his camp stool under his umbrella. They all kept dry and warm while the storm passed. At night they always stopped early enough to make good shelters. One night twenty of the men slept in the hollow trunk of a giant baobab tree.

David also believed part of his illness had been caused by the sudden change in diet. He had eaten only native food on the way west. This time he took some dried apricots and preserves. He also had flour. He baked bread in an oven made by turning a pot over a bed of coals. Warm bread and jam made a good breakfast.

He enjoyed the trip in perfect health.

David came across the ruins of a stone building. This had not been made by natives. He explored around the ruins. On one side lay a cross and broken bell. This was once a church. No inscription told who had built it. Someone had come here with great hopes of starting a missionary station. It had failed and fallen into ruin. The natives had forgotten its name.

That night as David tried to sleep, he felt a moment of gloom. What would become of his efforts? Would all that he had done fall into ruin as the church had? Would his trek across Africa be forgotten because he accomplished nothing worthy to be remembered. He opened the Bible. He came to this passage: "All power is given unto me in heaven and on earth; go ye, therefore, and teach all nations. . . . and lo, I am with you alway, even unto the end of the world."

The Bible strengthened his spirit. The moon had come up. David stepped outside his tent to take observations. He fixed the location of the church: latitude 15 degrees, 37 minutes, 22 seconds south, longitude 30 degrees, 32 minutes east.

David's goal now was the first civilized city, Tete. The local people said, "Ahead is a tribe with Mpende as chief. You should avoid him, for he hates white men."

"How should I go?" David asked.

"Cross the river and go on the other side," they suggested.

David asked them to take him across. The village elders talked among themselves. David and Sekwebu pretended to be ignorant of the language. But they knew the local dialect and could understand what the elders said. One of the elders said, "If we help him, Mpende may come after us. Send him on down the river. Tell him the next village will help them."

The expedition continued on Mpende's side of the river.

At sunrise, some of Mpende's people came nearby. They built a fire and waved charms over it. They shrieked and danced. David waited for a messenger from Mpende. Two men showed up. Behind them stood a large number of armed men.

David gave them a leg of an ox. David said, "Take it to Mpende."

After waiting a considerable time in suspense, two old men came. "Who are you?" they asked. From their aside conversations in their native tongue, David learned they thought him to be Portuguese.

"I am an Englishman," David said. One of the men recognized David as a member of the "friendly white tribe." He went back and persuaded Mpende to allow David to pass.

Mpende met with David. "The way to Tete is longer by following the river. It makes a great curve here. By crossing over and going overland you will save a great distance."

Sekwebu asked, "But who will take us across, if you do not?"

"You shall cross," Mpende said. He did everything he could to aid. Instead of an enemy, David had made a friend. He did it without giving a lot of gifts. They were now short of trade goods.

They came into a country with hunting laws. Half of the game killed had to be shared with the tribe that lived in the area. David's men succeeded in killing an elephant. They sent word back to the village. The half of the animal resting on the ground would belong to the local tribe. The other half would belong to the men who killed it.

The tribe brought a basket of corn, a fowl and a few strings of beads as a thank-you to David's men. "Eat it and be glad," they told David.

David's men made a feast. They camped around the elephant carcass for the night. An amazing number of hyenas gathered. They stayed just out of sight of the campfire light. They kept up their laughter-like bark all night.

"Why are the hyenas laughing?" David asked. He knew his men would have a good story to explain the laugh.

Sekwebu said, "They are laughing because we cannot take the whole elephant. 'We will have plenty to eat when you are gone,' they are saying."

They pushed on. Finally, they were near Tete. They camped eight miles from the village. Portuguese officers from Tete learned they were nearby. Commander Sicard and Lieutenant Miranda and some other soldiers marched to the camp. They arrived about two o'clock in the morning. They got the fire going and cooked breakfast for David.

David happily walked the eight miles to Tete. Commander Sicard gave David and his men lodging there. They were as generous on the east coast of Africa as they had been on the west.

It was still three hundred miles to Quilimane. But the route would be through civilized country under Portuguese control. David's men could either live at Tete until David returned, or they could try to make it back to Linyanti on their own. The men decided to stay.

"Most of my men would like to settle here," David told the commander.

Commander Sicard said, "I'll show them where they can build huts for themselves." He gave them a portion of land on which to grow their own food. They quickly set out to make a living for themselves. They hunted elephants for ivory and established a brisk trade in firewood.

David chose sixteen of the men who were good with canoes to take him and Lieutenant Miranda to the mouth of the Zambezi. Lieutenant Miranda then hired the sixteen men to carry government goods back up the river to Tete.

David crossed the final distance to Quilimane. The city had once been on a river, but a change of course left it twelve miles from the Zambezi. David arrived on May 20, 1856. The trip from Loanda to Quilimane, a trip across the continent, had taken twenty months.

While in Quilimane, he ran into George Fleming, the Cape Town trader, who had gone with him to Linyanti.

"Why are you here?" David asked.

It turned out that the businessman who employed George Fleming had sent him. George explained, "He directed me to meet you and deliver clothing, bedding and other comforts for your voyage home."

David looked around the great store of goods. "But this is far more than I would need."

George Fleming gave the rest of the story. "Should you fail to arrive, my orders were to proceed into the interior in quest of you."

David arranged passage home on the Oriental Steam Company's ship. They refunded his money for passage on the ship. David could not imagine why they would do so. He was an obscure person, a missionary to Africa. Why was everyone being so kind to him? Why had he not yet received any letters from Mary?

The way home had many adventures and disappointments. The ship was damaged during a storm so he had to await repairs. A telegram came while he was in Cairo and informed him that his father had died. His ship broke down again and he traveled overland across France and then by ship to England. He had intended to meet Mary at Southampton, but the new route put him at London. Finally, they had a happy reunion on December 11, 1856. Instead of two years, David had been away five years.

Mary had written a poem showing her love for him.

> *A hundred thousand welcomes, and it's time for you to come*
>
> *From the far land of the foreigner, to your country and your home*
>
> *Oh, long as we were parted, ever since you were away,*
>
> *I never passed an easy night, or knew an easy day.*
>
> *A hundred thousand welcomes! How my heart is gushing o'er*
>
> *With the love and joy and wonder just to see your face once more.*

Now he was at last reunited with his family. Almost every letter he had written to Mary had been lost along the way. The same happened to her letters.

Many of his friends came forward: Lord Playfair and James Young from his college days in Glasgow; Professor Owen and Doctor Bennet from his days of missionary training in London; Cotton Oswell, Colonel Thomas Steele and many others who had met him and Mary in Africa. Colonel Thomas Steele and Cotton Oswell had survived the Crimean War and now lived in England. Cotton Oswell had actually decided to settle down, get married and raise a family.

David found everyone wanted to hear about his adventures. Cotton Oswell said, "The Royal Geographical Society has requested your presence at their meeting next week."

Mary held an invitation. She said, "The London Missionary Society wishes for you to speak the next day."

Professor Owen said, "I'm a member of the Royal Society. We request the pleasure of your company at our next gathering." The Royal Society was a group of scientists. Only the best scientists in the world were allowed into that organization.

Doctor Bennet said, "The College of Physicians in Glasgow welcomes you, too."

David found every minute of his time taken in calling upon people to whom he had been sending letters.

The great men of the Geographical Society honored David Livingstone. John Herschel was there with a message from Mr. Thomas Maclear. When David stopped in Linyanti, he had asked Sekeletu to forward the observations to the Astronomer Royal at Cape Town. Sekeletu succeeded in getting the documents to Thomas Maclear. The Astronomer Royal then sent them to London with John Herschel.

John Herschel's father had discovered the planet Uranus. John Herschel had been in Cape Town to observe the southern skies. He reviewed David's observations.

John Herschel spoke to the Geographical Society. "I agree with Mr. Maclear. David Livingstone deserves every honor that is in our power to give. No explorer has recorded his path with such precision. You could go to any point across the entire continent, along Livingstone's track, and feel certain of your position."

The Royal Geographical Society awarded David a Gold Medal. David Livingstone had become the world's best known and most daring explorer.

The next day the London Missionary Society bestowed on him their highest praise. A few days later the Royal Society elected him a member. Like Professor Owen, he had become a famous scientist.

David traveled to Scotland to visit his family. The

Royal Faculty of Physicians in Glasgow welcomed him
as a new member. Only the best doctors and surgeons
were allowed into the organization.

In a short time he had been praised as an outstand-
ing explorer, missionary, scientist and doctor. No
individual had ever received so many honors in so
many different fields.

David visited home, back to Hamilton and to
Blantyre. He hugged his mother and spent the night
with her and his sisters. When they gathered around for
evening prayers, David saw his father's empty chair by
the fireplace. David suddenly burst into tears.

When he came back to England, John Murray, a
book publisher, called upon David. "Have you considered writing a book about your time in Africa?"

David said, "No. Who would be interested?
What would I have to pay to have it printed?"

John Murray said, "I am quite willing to take
upon myself the whole cost of publication, including
making the maps, illustrations and all the other expenses.
Normally, I give the author one half of the profit, but in
your case I will give a greater sum—two thirds."

David agreed to write the book but felt sorry for
Mr. Murray. The man intended to print 12,000 copies
of the book. It would take years for all of them to sell.
Mr. Murray would lose a fortune.

He rented an apartment in Chelsea to do the
writing. David set aside six months for the task. His
book would run to almost 700 pages, about 300,000
words. Although writing the book was hard work, this
time with his family was the happiest in his life.

As a break from the writing, he took his children
for walks into the nearby woods. He sneaked into a
thicket and set them searching for him. Suddenly he
plunged out at them and roared like a lion. He was

writing about the lion attack in his book. Mary looked on indulgently as her husband romped with the children.

David Livingstone was a lean man, sun-tanned. He still wore his battered peaked cap.

David wanted people to read his book and enjoy it. He wrote in a simple, popular language that everyone could understand. He filled the book with the sense of wonder he felt at the wonderful sights he saw in Africa. He explained that central Africa had fertile and well watered valleys. He encouraged young missionaries to make Africa their destination. He told Mary, "We are sowing seeds that will bud and blossom when we are gone."

Mary had become almost as famous as David. Long before David became a missionary, she had lived with her father and mother deep in Africa. With David she had traveled to Linyanti, far further than any other white woman. She had seen more and done more than almost any missionary except for David himself. The people who knew Mary, such as Thomas Steele and Cotton Oswell, expressed their great admiration for her.

Mary had lived in near poverty while away from David. Now she had more money. She still chose to dress in simple, humble clothes.

One day David took a recess from writing. He went to a reception at a photography exhibit at King's College. The best of English society came to the exhibit. The women who strolled through the Grand Hall dressed in their finest clothes.

Professor Owen came along later with Mary.

"Who is that dumpy woman with Professor Owen?" one of the high society women asked. "Look at that bonnet. It must be ten years out of style."

"She must be his cleaning woman," another woman said. "She wears a drab dress and ordinary plaid shawl."

"Quick, move away," the first woman said. "Professor Owen is bringing her this way. I don't want to be seen with a housemaid."

The second woman agreed. "I've come to see the great David Livingstone and his wonderful wife Mary."

David strode into the room and took Mary's hand. She stood at his side in the receiving line. The same people who earlier tried to avoid Mary now jostled for a place so they could claim to have met Dr. and Mrs. Livingstone.

After their outings, it was back to his writing table and the book manuscript. Mostly it was a matter of plowing through his notes and journals and rewriting them. He told the story as it happened without embellishments. What he saw and what he did were exciting enough.

"How is the writing going?" Mary asked.

"I'd rather cross Africa again on the back of a mean ox than write another book!" David said. "Writing is hard work. My respect for authors has increased a hundred fold!"

"Are the children bothering you?" she asked.

"Not at all," David said. "I learned in the cotton mill to study with all the noise and commotion."

David finished the book. He called it *Missionary Travels and Researches in South Africa.* He delivered the final pages of the manuscript to John Murray. David said, "I hope you will be able to sell enough copies to make a profit."

John Murray said gleefully, "It has already sold 13,800 copies—and it hasn't even left the printers!"

David looked stunned, "But you'd originally planned to print only 12,000 copies."

With satisfaction John Murray said, "I've already instructed the printers to start a second printing."

In quick succession, John Murray went back to the printing presses seven times. In only a few months the book sold 70,000 copies. David had written a best-seller!

He autographed some of the books and sent them to those who had helped him succeed. To his teacher at Blantyre he wrote: "To Mr. William MacSkimming with kindest remembrance of his pupil David Livingstone, London, 20 Nov 1857."

Editors now came to David begging for his writings about Africa. He found four articles that he had written at Cape Town before his great adventure. At that time no one would publish them. Now a magazine offered 400 pounds for the same material—four times his yearly salary.

When his book became a best-seller, David and Mary suddenly found themselves rich. After setting aside a sum to support his mother and help toward his children's education, he started to give the rest away— to young missionaries. He resigned from the London Missionary Society. They would no longer have the burden of providing him a salary.

Added to his other honors was this—he had become England's best known and most popular public speaker and author. As a young missionary student, he had been told he could not speak or write. Now he enjoyed being hailed as a best selling author. When he spoke, lecture halls filled to standing room only.

Because he planned to go back to Africa, the British government made a special government post for him. Dr. David Livingstone was appointed Her Majesty's Consul at Quilimane for the Eastern Coast of Africa. He put aside his plain midshipman's cap. He had worn it for sixteen years. Now he wore the counsel's cap. It looked the same except for a band of gold around it.

How else could he be honored? The answer came from Buckingham Palace at Westminster. Queen Victoria wished to meet with him.

David visited with Queen Victoria. He came without pomp or splendor, dressed in his usual fashion. He wore a black coat, blue trousers, and the new cap. They spoke for thirty minutes.

"Thank you for seeing me," David said. "When I visited the African tribes, they were amazed I had never met my chief. They asked if you are wealthy."

"What did you tell them?" Queen Victoria asked.

"I assured them that you are very wealthy," David said. "Then they asked how many cows you have."

Queen Victoria laughed. She asked, "What plans do you have now Doctor Livingstone?"

David said simply, "I shall return to Africa."

The expedition sailed from Liverpool on March 10, 1858. This time Mary went with him.

The Last Journey

Mary tried to hold back her tears as she boarded the train with David. She was leaving her three older children behind with friends in Scotland. Robert, Agnes and Thomas waved good-bye from the station platform. She meant for their last glimpse of her to be her smiling face. No, she could not do it. Tears streamed down her cheeks as the train chugged away.

David held her arm. She wiped away her tears. She had been born in Africa. As a young girl with her father and later with David, she had traveled thousands of miles by ox wagon across the wild countryside. Now she was going on another great adventure. She told her concerned husband, "I'll do my duty whatever betide."

David said, "At least we have one child with us." Six year old Oswell would visit his grandparents, the Moffats.

They sailed from Liverpool aboard the *Pearl*. It was a modern steamer with a screw propeller. Mary knew that her husband looked forward to this expedition. He believed it would be far easier than any of his others. The government paid him an adequate salary. They had provided him with better equipment. He had selected an experienced crew. He had money to buy anything else he needed.

Aboard the *Pearl* were the parts for another, smaller ship. It would be taken off and put together in Africa. David said, "It is a steam ship, especially designed to burn wood and draw a shallow draft. With it we will be able to sail up the Zambezi as far as Victoria Falls. I have named it the *Ma-Robert* in your honor." Ma-Robert was the name the African natives gave Mary.

As the voyage continued, Mary became desperately seasick. The cause was not only the sea, but also the fact that she was expecting another child. She was relieved to go ashore in Cape Town and visit with her mother and father. After much discussion, she decided to stay with them until the child was born.

On May 1, 1858 she stood on the dock and said good-bye to David. Once again she was in tears. As he sailed away, she waved her bonnet until the *Pearl* disappeared from her sight.

Mary and her folks did not leave Cape Town right away. They waited for Mary's brother, John Smith Moffat, and his bride, Emily, to come by a different ship from England. Finally, in August, the long train of ox wagons rolled out of Cape Town. Emily was expecting a child, too, so she and Mary gave one another support.

Mary's baby was born on November 16, 1858. She wrote a letter to David about the new member of the family, Anna Mary. She knew that a year or more would lapse before he received the news.

The next year Mary returned to England to put little Oswell in school. She had a happy reunion with Robert, Agnes and Thomas. While in England, mail from David caught up with her. He had not yet learned about Anna Mary's birth. From the letters, Mary could tell that David was desperately lonely.

About this time David sent one of his men to England to supervise building a new boat. The man was an engineer on the *Ma-Robert*. His name was George Rae, and he had been born in Blantyre, David's home town.

George Rae told Mary, "The expedition has been unlucky. David believed the *Pearl* would be able to go upstream to Tete. However, the Zambezi splits at its mouth into shallow channels. All are broad, shallow and clogged with mangroves and blocked by sand bars. It took us nearly four months to find a channel deep enough for the *Pearl* to pass. It could get no further than a mosquito-ridden island forty miles upstream. We unloaded the *Ma-Robert* and I put her together.

"The *Ma-Robert* turned out to be an inadequate ship. To keep her light, the hull was made of a sheet of iron only a tenth of an inch thick. Snags in the river punched holes in it. We had to constantly patch it and bail water. The steam engine was particularly inefficient. Wood cutters had to labor for a day and a half to keep her boilers fired for a day. When she got up a head of steam, she huffed and wheezed but did not go very fast. Canoes passed us. Finally, the *Ma-Robert* was replaced with a different ship, the *Pioneer*. Although more powerful, she sits too low in the water. We often run aground on sand bars."

Mary asked, "Were you able to take it up to Victoria Falls? I know David wanted to see the falls again."

Rae said, "That is where he is now. He took his Makololo men back to Linyanti. However, he didn't travel by ship. He had to go overland. As you know, during his earlier trek across Africa, he took Mpende's suggestion to shorten his trip by cutting cross country. In doing so he by-passed a great gorge on the Zambezi. The gorge is full of rapids. The river turns savage there, and neither the *Pioneer* nor any other ship could go beyond it."

"The other members of the expedition are at wits' end. We have all read David's book about his exciting travels. We joined the expedition for adventure, danger, and roughing it in the wilds. On the lower Zambezi we found only heat, humidity and mosquitoes. Everyone is irritable. Some have quit."

"David needs me," Mary said.

Rae agreed. "He is struggling."

Rae was in England supervising the building of engines for a third ship, the *Lady Nyasa*. This ship would be small enough to be taken apart, carried overland, and then put back together. In this way it could be carried past rapids.

"I'll go back with you," Mary decided. She would be leaving behind five children, the youngest only two.

Mary arrived at the mouth of the Zambezi aboard the British ship *Gorgon* on January 20, 1862. Far off in the distance near the mangrove trees, Mary saw a long, low ship, painted white. On the top deck stood a welcome sight. It was David, dressed in white trousers, frock coat and the naval cap. Mary detected not a touch of defeat in his straight, commanding stance.

The *Gorgon* ran up signal flags. "I have a steamship on board," the captain said. The ship was the little *Lady Nyasa*.

"Welcome news," The *Pioneer* responded.

The *Gorgon* ran up a second signal, "Wife on board."

"Accept my best thanks," David signaled back.

More than three years had passed since Mary waved good-bye to David at Cape Town. Now they were together again aboard the *Pioneer.* The ship throbbed slowly up the river. Aboard was a group of passengers intent on starting a new missionary station. The atmosphere was hot, steamy and filled with swarming insects. The crew and passengers suffered through sleepless nights because of swarms of mosquitoes. When rain fell, it left the air close and humid. The passengers and crew became more and more desperate.

In their happiness, David and Mary hardly noticed the adverse conditions. Mary had brought photographs of the children. David marveled at how much they had grown. He lingered over the photographs of Anna Mary, the little girl he had never seen. He asked about each child in turn, ending with the oldest Robert. Robert had always been a handful.

Mary said, "Robert has lost his way. He talks of going to the United States."

David said, "When they were young, I spent my energy in teaching the natives. I should have devoted a special portion of my time to play with my children."

Mary tried to console him. "Your days were long and tiring."

David nodded. "At the end of the day there was no fun left in me. I did not play with my little ones while I had them, and they soon sprang up in my absence, and now I have none."

The ship took them further north. Now they entered a wide, grassy savannah. The men went hunting.

The women put together picnic lunches and they ate delicious meals in the delightful country. David could hardly be happier.

The *Pioneer* had a dog, named Log. He was a bulldog, old and nearly blind. Once, while David and Mary ate in their cabin below deck, the dog fell through the skylight. He landed on Mary's plate. Both Mary and David laughed at the sudden interruption until tears rolled down their faces.

David said, "We should be more serious."

"Oh, no," Mary told him. "You must also be as playful as you have always been."

The *Pioneer* reached Shupanga. There David unloaded the *Lady Nyasa* for Rae to put together. Mary and David walked around the old town. They explored a stone house, long deserted. They stood in the shadow of a giant baobab tree and admired the view of the mountains in the distance. The canaries sang in the tree's ancient branches, and squirrels played around its trunk. David measured the size of the tree and entered it in his notebook.

Because of sickness among some of the passengers, David had to sail them back to the delta. There the *Pioneer* had engine trouble. Finally it was repaired. The delay in the sweltering heat struck Mary especially hard. By the time they made it back to Shupanga, she had become sick.

David carried her to the abandoned stone house. The men helped him make a bed—a mattress laid on wooden boxes. She had gotten sick before. David's medicine always revived her. This time it did not seem to be having an effect. Her temperature soared. She became delirious and thrashed about. Then she grew still. Her breath came in slow, painful rasps.

David called to her, "My dear, my dear, are you going to leave me?"

Mary died.

"She had been so strong," David murmured. "She was so much a part of me." He was left alone in the dark night. Outside he heard the howl of jackals and the low, mournful calls of water fowl on the river.

David's men hammered together a coffin while the sailors dug her grave. The place chosen for her burial was under the giant baobab. That night David measured the stars above the tree. He fixed its location so he could find it again even if the jungle took it over.

He looked through her belongings and found a prayer she had written. "Take me O Lord as I am and make me what thou wouldst have me be."

David wrote to his son Oswell. "With my tears running down my cheeks I have to tell you that poor dearly beloved Mama died last night about seven o'clock."

Soon the British government recalled the Zambezi expedition. David sailed the little *Lady Nyasa* across the Indian Ocean to Bombay, India. He refused to sell it in Africa. He did not want it to fall into the hands of African slave traders.

He arrived back in England on July 23, 1864. He went to Hamilton to visit his family. He saw Anna Mary for the first time. She was already five years old. Oswell was doing well, as was Agnes. She was a fine young woman who helped run David's household when he moved to England to write a book. Charles had never been strong, and the weather in Scotland had done nothing to improve his health. David looked into sending him to Egypt. The dryer climate might help.

His oldest son, Robert, had gone to the United States. The boy had enlisted in the Union Army under an assumed name, Rupert Vincent. He was wounded during a Civil War battle and taken prisoner. In a prisoner of war camp in North Carolina, Robert Livingstone died of his wounds.

David felt he should have done more to give Robert better direction. David said sadly, "We learn how to correct our errors only after the opportunity is gone."

The Royal Geographical Society asked David to return to Africa. David had traced out the route of the Zambezi. But sources of the Congo and the Nile were still unknown. David accepted their assignment. He would explore around Lake Nyasa and Lake Tanganyika. He would seek to unravel the sources of Africa's two great rivers.

David sailed to Bombay where he collected some of his trusted men, including Chuma and Susi. They were African natives that had sailed to Bombay with him on the *Lady Nyasa*. Susi had been a wood cutter on the ill-fated *Ma-Robert*. Chuma had been a slave that David freed from a slave driver. Chuma and Susi were devoted to David.

David took them to Zanzibar, an island off the east coast of Africa. It was a major trading center. There David put together a small expedition. He set out for the area around Lake Tanganyika. For a year or so, a few letters made it from him to the outside world. Then they stopped all together.

Several members of David's expedition appeared in Zanzibar. Their leader was a man named Musa. "David Livingstone is dead," Musa said. "He was attacked and killed near Lake Nyasa. We alone escaped."

The news spread to England. Flags flew at half staff. London newspapers published obituary notices.

Had the fearless African explorer finally reached the end of his road? The answer came from an unlikely person—an American newspaper reporter named Henry Morton Stanley.

He had been born in Wales as Henry Morton. His mother was an unmarried servant girl. She put him in a home for orphans. It was a workhouse and he endured bad treatment. He escaped when he turned sixteen years old. He sailed as a cabin boy to New Orleans. Although penniless, he fared better in the United States. In 1859 a dealer in cotton named Stanley befriended him. Henry Morton took the man's name as his own. He became Henry Morton Stanley.

When the Civil War began, the young Stanley joined the Confederate Army. In 1862, he switched sides and served on a Navy vessel of the Union forces.

After the Civil War, Stanley became a bold and successful roving reporter. He wrote about the American wild west for the St. Louis *Missouri Democrat* newspaper. Then he landed a job with the *Herald*, a big New York newspaper. The *Herald* sent him to Africa to cover fighting in Ethiopia. For the next two years he traveled throughout the Middle East and Europe.

His travels took him to Madrid, Spain. There he received a telegraph from the head of his paper James Gordon Bennett, Jr. The telegraph read: "Come to Paris on important business. Bennett."

Stanley quickly packed and boarded a train. He arrived at Paris the next night. He strode to Bennett's room in the Grand Hotel and knocked on the door.

"Come in," his boss said.

Stanley entered the room. The newspaper owner was in bed. The man asked, "Who are you?"

"My name is Stanley." Until then, Stanley had never met his boss.

"Ah, yes; sit down." He seemed impressed that Stanley had arrived so quickly. Bennett put on a robe. He peered closely at the young reporter. "I have important business on hand for you. Where do you think Livingstone is?"

"I really do not know, sir," Stanley replied.

Bennett demanded, "Do you think he is alive?"

"He may be and he may not be," Stanley answered.

Bennett said, "I think he is alive, and that he can be found. I am going to send you to find him."

"What!" Stanley said. "Do you really think I can find Doctor Livingstone? The British have sent out four expeditions with the best explorers they could muster. All came back empty. You mean for me to go to central Africa?"

"Yes. You shall go and find him wherever you may hear that he is. Get what news you can of him. Perhaps, he may be in want. Take enough with you to help him should he require it. Of course, you will act according to your own plans. Do what you think best— but find Livingstone!"

"It will be expensive," Stanley said.

Bennett dismissed the cost with a wave of the hand. "Draw a thousand pounds now. When you have gone through that, draw another thousand, and so on. But, find Livingstone."

Stanley sat silently, thinking. It was an incredible opportunity, but a daunting task. Stanley had been to northern Africa and did not enjoy the visit. He resolved to go to Africa, find Livingstone if he were alive, write his dispatches and quickly get out. He would not linger in Africa. The country held no charms for him!

Bennett said, "It will take some time for you to research the best way to go about locating Livingstone and to outfit an expedition. While you are doing that, I have some other assignments for you. Go to Egypt to report on the opening of the Suez Canal. Because of the canal, travelers from all over the world will be coming to Egypt. Write about tourist attractions on the upper Nile."

After taking care of his other assignment, Stanley finally arrived at Zanzibar.

On the island, he spent a lot of money to outfit the expedition. He signed bank draft after bank draft. He spent 5000 pounds and bought six tons of equipment and supplies. Should J. G. Bennett decide not to honor the checks, Stanley would need to disappear into Africa to avoid going to jail.

Stanley found two people who knew Livingstone. One was Francis Webb, the American Consul. The other was John Kirk, the British Consul. He had served with Livingstone on the Zambezi expedition.

Stanley visited John Kirk. The British Consul showed off his new elephant rifle. He told in long and boring detail his many hunting expeditions. Finally he touched upon his travels with Livingstone.

"Yes, Dr. Kirk," Stanley asked. "Doctor Livingstone, where do you think he is now?"

John Kirk answered with a shrug. "That is very difficult to answer. Of one thing I am sure, nobody has heard anything of him for over two years."

Stanley pressed for a more definite answer. "Do you think he is alive or dead?"

John Kirk said, "I should fancy that he must be alive."

Francis Webb, the American Consul, and his wife invited Stanley into their home. They let him store his expedition goods under canvas in their yard. Francis

Webb surveyed the tons of supplies. He said, "This is the largest expedition I've seen by far."

Stanley confessed, "I am totally ignorant of the interior. It is difficult to know what I need."

Stanley decided to head straight for Ujiji, on the eastern shore of Lake Tanganyika. It was a center of trade around the lakes in that part of Africa. Many people passed through that town. Even if he did not find the famous explorer there, he might find recent information about the explorer's whereabouts.

At first Stanley's expedition had easy going. The scenery was as beautiful and tame as an English park. Then they came to a swamp. For five days they slogged through water and mud. One of his key men caught African fever. Then one of his Arab helpers.

Then Stanley got sick. As soon as he shrugged off the fever, he came down with dysentery. His weight fell from 170 pounds to 130 pounds. Stanley kept up a blistering pace. They reached Tabora, the Arab's central African capital, in record time. The trek of 525 miles took a mere 84 days.

Stanley asked about Livingstone. The natives at Tabora had heard of him. "He is old," they said. "He has white hair on his face, and he is sick."

Stanley pushed on. On November 9, 1871, he made camp with Ujiji only a few hours away. The next morning he woke and made ready to march into the village. He dressed in fresh clothes, white flannels, well-polished boots, and his pith helmet. His men formed a long line. They lifted their loads and marched along with renewed vigor. Stanley marched at the head. A man behind him carried the flag of the United States. They fired their guns in the air to announce their approach. This let the town know they came in peace— they were not trying to sneak up on them.

Crowds gathered and cheered. They had never seen anything like Stanley's expedition.

Susi heard the commotion. He and Chuma thought surely medicine and supplies would be waiting for them at Ujiji. But they were not. The supplies and medicines had been sold by the man sent from Zanzibar to deliver and guard it. There had been no mail either. Susi and Chuma, two of David Livingstone's native companions, did not know what to do.

When he heard the noise, Susi ran outside. As the long line of bearers came into view, he marveled at the size of the caravan. He saw bales of goods, boxes, trade goods, huge kettles, cooking pots and tents. The long line of men kept coming. He could see the man in front. He darted out to meet the stranger. "It's an Englishman! I see him," he yelled back to Chuma.

People of Ujiji began blowing on horns and beating drums in welcome. They flocked to surround the newcomers. Over the heads of the people Susi could see the flag more carefully. It was not the British flag. It was the Stars and Stripes of America.

Susi elbowed his way through the excited crowd. He addressed the leader in English, "Good morning, sir!"

"Who are you?" Stanley asked.

But Susi had dashed off in great excitement. He ran into the hut.

Stanley walked forward. Susi, Chuma and a group of men stood in a respectful semi-circle. A man hobbled out of the hut. The man had a white beard. He was thin and dressed in a red shirt. His gray trousers were worn and frayed. He wore a battered blue cap decorated with a faded gold band.

Stanley wanted to run to meet the man. Instead,

he hid his excitement. He walked forward with great
dignity.

Stanley raised his hat. "Dr. Livingstone, I pre-
sume."

The other man nodded and raised his hat. "Yes."

David Livingstone in Today's World

The British had told Stanley that David Livingstone was a reserved man who would give him a cool reception. Instead, David Livingstone smiled warmly and greeted the young newspaper man as an equal.

"Come into the shade," David said.

Stanley said, "I have a bag of mail for you."

David put the bag at his feet. He turned his bright hazel eyes to Stanley. David said, "Tell me news of the outside world."

Incredible! Stanley thought. *I've come all this way to hear about his adventures. Instead, he wants to hear what I have to say.* Stanley described all the great events of the last five years. "The Suez Canal has opened. A transatlantic telegraph cable has been successfully laid. Messages can be flashed from New York to London in the blink of an eye."

David asked, "Was William Thomson one of the electrical engineers?"

"More than that," Stanley said. "William Thomson had been called in to solve some design problems of the submerged telegraph line. He then supervised the laying of the cable across the Atlantic."

David said simply, "We went to school in Glasgow together."

Then David began telling the story of his time in Africa. Henry Stanley listened in great admiration. He had never met a man so calm, so comfortable, so instantly likable. He forgot to bring out his reporter's notebook. He did not care. He merely wanted to listen, to soak up the words of this great man.

They shared a meal prepared jointly by their cooks. They continued to talk.

Stanley asked about Musa. "He claimed you were dead."

"Musa and his men abandoned me years ago," David said. "They had been such thieves, I was not sorry to see them go."

Stanley told him what happened. "Musa came to Zanzibar and reported you dead. He had a reputation as a thief and liar. Your friends refused to believe the story. They found some porters who had seen you alive well after Musa had left you. When the truth came out, the sultan sentenced Musa to eight months in jail."

David said, "For every man like Musa there are those like Susi and Chuma who have faithfully followed me."

David told how Chuma had come to join the expedition. "During the Zambezi expedition we came across a gang of captives. They were held by stout wooden poles with forked ends into which their necks were fastened. The end of each pole was lashed onto the slave immediately behind. When the slave raiders saw us they darted off into the forest.

"We sawed the men free. Soon they were cooking a meal over a fire fueled with the slave poles. Chuma was one of those we freed. That was in 1861. He has been with me ever since--for ten years."

Within a few days, Stanley had written the story of Livingstone's travels in his notebook. Now it was time to march back to civilization and file his story. He had a scoop like no other. Yet he hesitated.

He could not bear to leave this gentle man. Henry Stanley never had a father. Here, in the heart of Africa, he found the father he never had. Livingstone, in turn, seemed happy to look upon the young reporter as a son.

Throughout his life Henry Stanley felt a strong need to prove himself. Livingstone's acceptance made him feel at ease. He wrote in his notebook: "I have come to entertain an immense respect for myself and begin to think of myself as somebody."

Henry Stanley called in his porters and began unloading his store of goods. He divided his clothes in two heaps and gave one to David. He went through his medicine chest and divided it. He shared all that he had.

"I am a little ashamed at having nothing worthy of your generosity," David said.

Henry Stanley waved away David's thanks. "I am the one being blessed," he said. He still could not leave David. He suggested they go exploring together. "We could take a canoe along the shores of Lake Tanganyika together."

Within a week after their meeting at Ujiji, they set off. David had arrived at Ujiji about four days before Stanley. He had been weak and sick. With Stanley's care he soon recovered. They spent four weeks exploring the lake. David called the little expedition a "picnic."

They took two more weeks to write their journals, letters and dispatches. David turned over not only his letters to Stanley, but also his precious journals. David said, "I've been writing letters everywhere I go. At one of my earlier visits to Ujiji, I wrote 42 letters."

Henry Stanley said, "None of your letters were ever seen."

"I feared as much," David said. "Individual Arabs have been friendly with me. But they know my opposition to slavery. When they find pouches of my letters, they destroy them."

It was time for Stanley to leave. He tried to talk David into coming home with him. David tried to talk Stanley into staying longer. In the end, David agreed to go with Stanley part way, to Unyanyembe.

"I'll send you supplies and honest porters from Zanzibar," Henry Stanley said. "Stay in Unyanyembe until they arrive."

They arrived at Unyanyembe. David agreed to wait there for Stanley to send supplies. He walked with Stanley to the crest of a hill. It was time for Stanley to leave. They shook hands, their faces filled with emotion. Tears welled up. David Livingstone, the fearless African explorer, wept as they parted.

The trip to the coast would normally take 90 days. "March!" Stanley told his men. "We shall be there in 40 days." He reached his destination in 35 days.

Stanley wrote to the *Herald* about his days with David Livingstone. "For four months and four days I lived with him in the same house, or in the same boat, or in the same tent, and I never found a fault in him. I am a man of quick temper and often without sufficient cause. With Livingstone I never had cause for

resentment, but each day's life with him added to my admiration."

David sent a letter to the *Herald*. His thoughts were on the terrible slave trade that he observed in this part of Africa. He wrote, "All I can say in my solitude is, may Heaven's rich blessing come down on everyone—American, English, Turk—who will help heal this open sore of the world."

Stanley kept his promise. He spent some more of J. G. Bennett's money and sent supplies and men back to David. Jacob Wainwright was one of the men. He had been educated in India. Unlike Susi and Chuma he could read and write. But like Susi and Chuma, he quickly formed a strong bond of loyalty to David Livingstone.

David began exploring again. He looked healthy. He had gained weight and shrugged off the sickness. But he was also sixty years old. After a year of struggling through the swamps around the lakes he became sick and weak once again. His followers had to carry him on a litter.

At the village of Chief Chitambo they built a hut
for him. David followed a routine each night. He would
wind his precision watch, write in his journals, and pray
before going to sleep.

Susi, Chuma and Wainwright grew worried.
David had become too weak to wind the watch. He
wrote only a few words in his journal. For the last four
days he had not made any entries. They appointed a
young boy, Majwara, to wait outside his door. Should
David need anything, the boy would call for help.

About 4 a.m. on May 1, 1873, the boy came for
Susi and Chuma. They went back to the hut and stood
at the entrance. A single candle burned. By the flickering
light, they saw David out of his cot and kneeling with
his head buried in his hands upon the pillow.

David did not stir. There was no sign of breathing.
Slowly, one of the men walked forward. The man
touched his cheek. He was cold. Sometime during the
night, David had died as he prayed.

Susi, Chuma and Jacob Wainwright talked together. What to do? The body and David's belongings
should be returned to England they decided. Jacob
Wainwright wrote out a careful inventory of all David's
clothes, supplies and scientific instruments. Every
item would be returned to England. No one could
accuse them of plundering David's possessions.

They prepared the body for the journey. It was
embalmed, packed in salt and wrapped in a cylinder of
tree bark. Chuma coated the bark with tar to make it
waterproof. Then he wrapped it in canvas to be carried
below a pole between two men.

The tribes along the route had a great superstitious
fear of dead bodies. They would have refused to let the
men pass with a body. Chuma made the container look
like a bolt of cloth. No one would know they carried a
corpse.

Chuma had removed David's heart and buried it in a tin box under a Mvula tree. Jacob Wainwright carved an inscription to mark the place.

Now the men began the incredible journey. It was a thousand miles through dangerous territory to the coast. The courage and devotion they showed has become an epic story in itself. They did reach the coast. They did turn over the body and all of David's belongings and scientific instruments to the British.

Jacob Wainwright was invited to go back to England with the body. Chuma and Susi followed some months later.

When the body arrived in England, there was some question whether it was actually that of David Livingstone. Doctors examined the mangled left shoulder and broken bones from the lion attack. They settled all doubt. This was David Livingstone.

On April 18, 1874, a day of national mourning, Livingstone was given a state funeral at Westminster Abbey. Accompanying the body were Cotton Oswell, Thomas Steele, James Young, John Kirk, Henry Stanley and Jacob Wainwright. Present, too, was Robert Moffat.

The headstone is flush on the floor in the center of the nave of the church, between the tomb of the unknown soldier and the monument to Isaac Newton. It is black marble with gold writing.

What did David Livingstone accomplish to deserve such a position of high honor?

As an explorer and scientist he mapped a trail from one side of Africa to the other. He discovered the source of the Zambezi and found numerous lakes. He traveled 30,000 miles in Africa. All along the way he recorded in accurate detail the weather, water courses, elevation, location and commercial possibilities of the native resources. His detailed journals have set a standard for other explorers to match.

As a doctor he brought the latest scientific methods to the natives deep in Africa. He used chloroform as a pain killer during surgery long before some doctors in civilized countries fully realized its potential. He accepted the germ theory of disease and began boiling water to kill microorganisms while other doctors still debated whether germs caused disease.

As a writer and public speaker he convinced others to follow in his footsteps. Henry Stanley said, "I was converted by him, although he had not tried to do it." Henry Stanley, the man who disliked Africa, spent the rest of his life exploring those areas David had left untouched.

Cotton Oswell said, "If ever a man carried out the Scriptural injunction to take no thought for tomorrow, that man was David Livingstone."

Henry Stanley said, "I grant he is not an angel, but he approaches to being that as near as the nature of a living man will allow. His gentleness never forsook him; his hopefulness never deserted him. Whenever he began to laugh, there was a contagion about it that compelled me to imitate him."

As a missionary he lived a life that spoke as loud as his words. Within two months of his burial the Sultan of Zanzibar issued an order to outlaw the export of slaves from his domain. The slave trade ended.

David Livingstone's popularity with the people of Africa increased as the years passed. Africans have opened museums in his honor and issued stamps to commemorate his deeds. His home in Kolobeng is preserved. There is a town in Africa named Livingstone and another one named Blantyre after where he was born.

Ten years after David's death a traveler came across Chief Sechele, David's first Christian convert.

The great chief still lived a Christian life. He had gained a thorough knowledge of the Bible. He preached the Gospel and befriended missionaries. He eagerly read all he could about his famous friend.

David Livingstone found a way into the heart of Africa and into the hearts of Africans.

BIBLIOGRAPHY

John Bierman, *Dark Safari, The Life Behind the Legend of Henry Morton Stanley* (New York: Alfred A. Knopf, 1990).

W. Garden Blaikie, *The Personal Life of David Livingstone* (New York: Negro University Press, A division of Greenwood Publishing Corp., 1969. Originally published in 1880 by Fleming H. Revell Company).

Timothy Holmes, ed., *David Livingstone: Letters & Documents, 1841-1871* (Bloomington, Indiana: Indiana University Press, 1990).

Elspeth Huxley, *Livingstone and his African Journeys* (New York: Saturday Review Press, 1974).

Tim Jeal, *Livingstone* (New York: G. P. Putnam's Sons, 1973).

Judith Listowel, *The Other Livingstone* (New York: Charles Scribner's Sons, 1974).

David Livingstone, *Missionary Travels and Researches in South Africa* (New York: Harper & Brothers Publishers, 1858).

David and Charles Livingstone, *Narrative of an Expedition to the Zambesi and its Tributaries* (New York: Harper & Brothers Publishers, 1866).

Oliver Ransford, *David Livingstone: The Dark Interior* (New York: St. Martin's Press, 1978).

Robert I. Rotberg, ed., *Africa and its Explorers, Motives, Methods, and Impact* (Cambridge, Massachusetts: Harvard University Press, 1970).

George Seaver, *David Livingstone: His Life and Letters* (New York: Harper & Brothers Publishers, 1957).

194   DAVID LIVINGSTONE

Fredrika Shumway Smith, *Stanley, African Explorer*
    (Skokie, Illinois: Rand McNally & Company,
    1968).
Jack Simmons, *Livingstone and Africa* (New York:
    The Macmillan Company, 1955).
Peter J. Westwood, *David Livingstone, His Life and
    Work as Told Through the Media of Postage
    Stamps and Allied Material* (Edinburgh,
    Scotland: Jamieson & Munro, 1986).

INDEX

Africa, 1, 2, 15, 21, 23, 26-30, 32, 36, 39-43, 45, 47, 48, 52, 53, 59, 63, 65, 67-70, 77, 79, 80, 84, 85, 88, 91, 93, 95, 100, 102, 104, 106, 107, 110, 111, 116-123, 125, 128, 131, 136, 141, 147, 148, 158, 160-170, 172, 175-191

Aldersgate Street Dispensary, 27

Algeria, Africa, 40

anatomy, 27

Anderson, Arthur, 6, 14, 15

Anderson's College, Glasgow, 9, 104

anesthetic, see chloroform

Angola, Africa, 141

army ants, 147

Astronomer Royal, see Maclear, Thomas

Atlantic Ocean, 23, 39, 40, 128, 149, 184

Baba (native helper), 63, 64, 75, 78-80

Bakhatla (Chief Moseealele's tribe, smelted iron), 56, 58, 59

Bakwena (Chief Sechele's tribe), 52, 53, 90

baobab tree, 48, 100, 155, 157, 174, 175

Bedingfeld, Commander Norman, 144

Bennet, Dr. Risdon, 27, 76, 103, 162, 163

Bennett, James Gordon, 177, 178, 187

Blantyre, Africa, 191

Blantyre, Scotland, 2, 5, 6, 9, 17, 28, 104, 164, 167, 171

Boers, 39, 119, 120, 121, 122

Bombay, India, 175, 176

botany, 27

Bothwell estate, 10

Brazil, South America, 37

Broomielaw Quay, Glasgow, Scotland, 29

Bubi, Chief, 60, 62, 63, 65, 90

Buckingham Palace, 168

Bushman, 47, 54, 97, 98, 110, 111, 112

canal (to water crops), 62, 71

Canton, China, 7

Cape Observatory, South Africa, 129

Cape of Good Hope, South Africa, 39

Cape Town, 39, 43, 46, 65, 68, 83, 84, 88, 102, 105, 108, 116, 118, 119, 120, 121, 145, 151, 161, 163, 167, 170, 173

Cassange (Portuguese outpost, Western Africa), 141, 142, 145, 146, 147, 148

Cecil, Richard, 20-22

Charing Cross Dispensary, London, 27

Chiboque (Chief Njambi's warlike tribe), 137, 138

China, 7, 8, 15, 21, 24

Chipping Ongar, 20

Chitambo, Chief (chief of village where David Livingstone died), 187

chloroform, 102, 103, 190

Chobe River, 112, 124, 126

Chonuane (Chief Sechele's first village), 52, 86, 88, 92

Christian convert, first, 91, 191, see also Chief Sechele

Chuma (assistant, freed slave), 176, 181, 184, 185, 187-189

church building, abandoned, 157

Civil War, American, 176, 177

Clyde River, Scotland, 9
collecting plants, 5, 14
collecting scientific samples, 28,
    54, 70, 87
College of Physicians, 163
Congo River, 40, 176
cotton mill, 2, 3, 10, 14, 17, 45,
    84, 104, 121, 166
Crimean War, 148, 162
de Abrao, Sergeant Cypriano, 141
Dick, Dr. Thomas, 6, 7
Dilolo, Lake (African watershed),
    149
Donaldson, Captain (of the
    George), 30, 32-36, 38, 39
drought, 86, 90, 91, 102, 109, 115
Dutch colonists, 119, see also
    Boers
Dutch East India Company, 39, 84
Edinburgh, Scotland, 4, 27
Edwards, Rogers, 49-51, 53-58,
    60, 65-67, 70, 76, 81, 82
Egypt, 40, 58, 88, 175, 179
elephants, 43, 51, 160
Ferguson, Fergus, 19
Fleming, George (native trader for
    Cape Town merchant), 119,
    122, 124, 161
Forerunner (mail ship, sank with
    Livingstone's journal), 146,
    148
Gabriel, Edmund (British Com-
    missioner at Loanda), 142-146,
    151
George, 30, 32, 35, 43, 123, 161
Glasgow, Scotland, 9-11, 13, 14,
    16, 17, 19, 20, 22, 28, 29, 104,
    162-164, 184
Gold Medal, 104, 163
Gorgon, 172, 173
Gospel, 6, 8, 16, 21, 30, 47, 59,
    66, 70, 77, 82, 92, 93, 103,
    112, 191
Graham, Dr. Thomas, 13
Greenwich, England, 33
Griqua Town, South Africa, 48, 49
Gutzlaff, Karl (missionary to
    China), 7, 8, 15, 24

Hamilton (elderly missionary), 49,
    65
Hamilton Church, 5-9, 14, 15, 16
Hamilton, Scotland, 151, 164, 175
Herald (New York newspaper),
    177, 186, 187
Herbal, 5
Herschel, John, 163
High Street, Glasgow, 13
Hippocrates, 88
hippopotamus, 125
honey guide, 64
"Hundred Thousand Welcomes,
    A" (Mary's poem), 162
Hunterian Museum, 27
hyenas, 159, 160
India, 15, 21, 39, 40, 53, 84, 187
Indian Ocean, 39, 145, 149, 175
*Indigenous Plants of Lanarkshire,
    The,* 5
Inglis, Walter (missionary
    student), 21
iron smelting, 58
Josephus, 88
journal, David Livingstone's, 28,
    46, 47, 64, 88, 93, 116, 129,
    131, 140, 148, 166, 186, 187,
    190
Kalahari Desert, 23, 39, 41, 47,
    53, 85, 93, 95, 122, 123
Kanyata (native guide on explora-
    tion east to Quilimane), 151
Kasai River, 149
Kelvin, Lord, see Thomson,
    William
Kirk, John (British Consul at Zan-
    zibar), 179, 189
Kolobeng, 92-95, 99, 100, 102,
    108, 109, 116, 119, 121, 190
Kuruman, 23, 26, 28, 29, 30, 41,
    43-49, 51, 59, 60, 63, 65,
    67-70, 77, 79, 80, 82, 84, 88,
    93, 95, 102, 105, 108, 110,
    119, 120, 151
Lady Nyasa, 172, 174, 175, 176
Lancet (medical journal), 28
language problems, 66
Latin, 4, 19, 20, 37, 94

Lechulatebe, Chief, 107
Lemue, Rev. Prosper, 80
Lepelole (Chief Bubi's village),
60, 61, 63, 65, 71, 90
Light Brigade, 148
Linyanti, 114, 116, 119, 126, 128,
129, 131, 145, 146, 148, 150
151, 160, 161, 163, 165, 172
lion attack, 1, 51, 71, 72, 73, 78,
189
Livingstone, Africa (town), 190
Livingstone, David
answers question about duties
of a Christian missionary, 16;
answers question about marriage, 16; birth, 2; death, 187;
doctor, 8, 27, 57, 102, 164,
190; explorer, 46, 53, 95, 104,
110, 128, 145, 151, 163, 176,
189; marriage, 80; missionary,
8, 20, 52, 89, 91, 103, 112,
127, 135, 163, 190; scientist,
5, 7, 28, 87, 103, 122, 163;
speaker, 19, 22, 167, 190;
writer, 119, 164, 166, 167, 190
Livingstone, family
Livingstone, Agnes (mother),
3, 6, 29, 167
Livingstone, Agnes (sister),
10, 29
Livingstone, Agnes (daughter),
92, 103, 171, 175
Livingstone, Anna Mary
(daughter), 170, 171, 173, 175
Livingstone, Charles (brother),
10, 29
Livingstone, Charles (son),
175
Livingstone, Elizabeth (daughter), 108, 109
Livingstone, Janet (sister), 10,
13, 14, 29, 103
Livingstone, John (brother),
10, 14, 29
Livingstone, Mary Moffat
(wife), 26, 27, 77-84, 86-90,
92, 95, 102-111, 113, 115,
117, 121, 143-146, 156, 161,

162, 165-175
Livingstone, Neil (father), 3, 5,
8, 9, 18, 19, 28
Livingstone, Robert (son), 92,
103, 171, 173, 175
Livingstone, Thomas (son),
102, 103, 171
Livingstone, William Oswell
(son), 115, 169, 171, 175
Loanda (Portuguese town on west
coast of Africa), 128, 129,
141-143, 145, 148, 150, 153,
157, 161
locusts and wild honey, 64, 65
lodging at cotton mill, 10
London Missionary Society, 15,
16, 18, 19, 24, 28, 30, 60, 116,
117, 143-145, 162, 163, 167
London, 16, 19, 20, 22, 24, 27, 28,
30, 76, 84, 88, 107, 121, 129,
161-163, 167, 176, 183
Mababe (Makololo town on
Chobe River), 112, 113
Mabotsa, 1, 65, 66, 69, 70-72, 79,
81-84, 86
Maclear, Thomas (Astronomer
Royal), 118, 129, 132, 151,
163
MacSkimming, William (teacher
employed by Blantyre cotton
mill), 3, 4, 167
"magic" lantern, 129, 135
Majwara, 187
Makhari (Chief Sechele's wife
who had no family), 91
Makololo (Chief Sebituane's
people), 95, 102, 110, 112,
114, 116, 119, 125, 126,
133-135, 139, 142, 144, 146,
150, 151, 172
malaria, 134, 135, 139, 141-143,
157
Ma-Mochisane, Chief (daughter of
Chief Sebituane), 114, 126,
127
Ma-Nenko (assigned to take Livingstone's expedition to Chief
Shinte), 132-134, 150

Ma-Robert (ship), 170, 171, 176

Ma-Sebele (escaped sack of Kolobeng), 119, 120

matlametlo, 48

Ma-Unku (wife of Chief Sebituane), 114

measuring latitude and longitude, 33, 100, 119

Mebalwe (native assistant missionary), 46, 47, 49, 50, 52, 60, 62, 63, 67, 69, 72, 73, 75, 78, 79, 106, 120, 122

medicine men, 60, 61, 62, 113

mirage, 98

Miranda, Lieutenant, 160

Missionary Travels and Researches in South Africa (book by David Livingstone), 166

Moffat, Emily (Mary Livingstone's sister-in-law), 170

Moffat, John Smith, 170

Moffat, Robert, 23, 24, 26, 27, 29, 30, 47-49, 60, 65-70, 77, 80, 89, 113, 120, 151, 189

Moffat, Annie (wife's sister), 26

Mohorisi (native guide), 133, 139, 140, 151

Moir, John, 6, 8, 9, 16

Moore, Joseph (missionary student), 20, 21, 22

Morocco, Africa, 40

Moseealele (chief of the Bakhatla tribe), 56

Moselele (chief of Mabotsa), 65, 70, 71, 75, 76

Mpende, Chief, 158, 159, 172

Mpepe (brother of Sekeletu), 126, 127

Murray, Mungo, 94, 95, 97, 104, 166, 167

Musa (betrayed Livingstone), 176, 184

native missionaries, 47, 69

navigation, 32, 34, 93, 129

Netherlands Missionary Society, 7

Newton, Isaac, 20, 189

Ngami, Lake, 85, 93, 95, 98-100,

104, 107, 109, 110

Niger River, 40

Nile River, 40, 41, 176, 179

Njambi, Chief, 137-139

North Celestial Pole, 33

Nyasa, Lake, 176

Opium War, 24

Orange River crossing, 45

Orange River, 39, 43, 44, 45, 48

ostrich, measuring speed, 122

Oswell, William Cotton, 82-85, 93-100, 102, 104-106, 108, 109, 110-117, 126, 145, 148, 162, 165, 189, 190

Owen, Richard, 27, 28, 54, 87, 103, 145, 162, 163, 165, 166

ox-wagon, 43, 44

Paradise Lost, 4

Paris Evangelical Society, 80

Park, Mungo, 40

passport, 141

Paul (native assistant missionary), 49, 60, 63

Pearl, 169-171

Philosophy of a Future State, 6

Pilgrim's Progress, 4, 89

Pioneer, 171-174

Pires, Colonel, 146, 148

Pitsane (Makololo head man on expedition), 133, 139, 149, 151

Playfair, Lyon, 12, 162

poison arrows, 54

Polaris, 33

Pomare (native assistant), 43, 45, 50, 51, 57, 59

Port Elizabeth, South Africa, 23, 43, 48, 59

Portuguese (in Africa), 39, 40, 140, 160

Portuguese (in South America), 37

Prime Meridian, 33

Psalms, 18, 29

Punch, 28, 88

quadrant, 34

Queen Victoria, 121, 153, 168

Quilimane, 145, 151, 160, 161, 168

quinine, 108, 143
Rae, George, 171, 172
rain making, 61
Rio de Janeiro, Brazil, 35, 36
Ross, William, 30, 35, 36, 45, 49
Rotten Row Apartment, Glasgow, 11
Royal College of Surgeons, London, 27, 28, 145
Royal Faculty of Physicians, 164
Royal Geographical Society, 104, 145, 162, 163, 176
Royal Society of Edinburgh, 13
Royal Society, 162, 163
Rudiments of the Latin Tongue, 4
Sahara Desert, 23, 40, 41
Scotland, 2, 6, 7, 23, 26, 27, 29, 77, 151, 163, 169, 175
Sebituane (chief of the Makololo), 53, 95, 102, 105, 106, 107-110, 112-114, 125, 126
Sechele, Chief (first Christian convert), 52, 53, 59, 82, 88-95, 102, 103, 106, 107, 108, 119, 120-122, 191
Sehamy (native assistant), 50, 51, 63, 64
Sekeletu, Chief (son of Sebituane), 126-128, 133, 145, 146, 150-153, 163
Sekwebu (native guide), 151, 157-160
sextant, 100, 119, 129, 153
Shaka Zulu, 156
Shinte, Chief, 132-137, 145, 150
Shobo (Bushman guide), 110-112
Sicard, Commander (of Tete), 160
Sichuana (African language), 50, 60, 66, 89, 104, 110
Sierra Leone, 40
Sinbad (riding ox), 128, 130, 134, 136, 149, 150
slave traders, 116, 127, 134, 142, 175, 184, 187
slavery, 24, 135, 186
smoke that sounds, smoke that thunders, see Victoria Falls
South America, 36

South Pacific, 15
Stanley, Henry Morton, 177-190
Steele, Thomas, 148, 162, 165, 189
storm at night, 152
storm at sea, 35
Suez Canal, 179, 183
Susi (native assistant), 176, 181, 184, 187-189
Tahiti, 21
Tanganyika, Lake, 176, 180, 185
Tete, 158-160, 171
Thomson, William, 12, 104, 184
Three Journeys along the Coast of China, 8
Timbuktu, 40
Times of London (newspaper), 148
Tripoli, 40
tsetse fly, 123, 146, 150, 152
Ujiji, 180, 181, 185, 186
Unyanyembe, 186
Vaal River, 68
Victoria Falls, 115, 151, 153, 170, 171
Vincent, Rupert, 176, see Livingstone, Robert (son)
Wainwright, Jacob, 187, 188, 189
wait-a-bit thorn bush, 43
waterfall, 24, 38, see also Victoria Falls
watershed of Africa, 149
Watt, D. G. (missionary student), 21
Webb, Francis (American Consul at Zanzibar), 179
West Indies, 15, 24, 26
Westminster Abbey, 20, 189
Young, James, 12, 13, 145, 162, 189
Zambezi River, 40, 100, 115, 128, 149, 151, 160, 161, 170-172, 175, 176, 179, 184, 189
Zanzibar, 176, 179, 181, 184, 186, 190
Zouga River, 98, 99, 115
Zouga, nickname for William Cotton Livingstone (son), 115

SOWERS SERIES

Abigail Adams by Evelyn Witter
Johnny Appleseed by David Collins
Robert Boyle by John Hudson Tiner
William Jennings Bryan by Robert Allen
George Washington Carver by David Collins
Christopher Columbus by Bennie Rhodes
George Frideric Handel by Charles Ludwig
Mahalia Jackson by Evelyn Witter
Stonewall Jackson by Charles Ludwig
Johannes Kepler by John Hudson Tiner
Francis Scott Key by David Collins
Jason Lee by Charles Ludwig
Robert E. Lee by Lee Roddy
Abraham Lincoln by David Collins
David Livingstone by John Hudson Tiner
Samuel F. B. Morse by John Hudson Tiner
Isaac Newton by John Hudson Tiner
Florence Nightingale by David Collins
Louis Pasteur by John Hudson Tiner
Samuel Francis Smith by Marguerite Fitch
Billy Sunday by Robert Allen
Teresa of Calcutta by D. Jeanene Watson
George Washington by Norma Cournow Camp
Daniel Webster by Robert Allen
Noah Webster by David Collins
Susanna Wesley by Charles Ludwig
The Wright Brothers by Charles Ludwig